THE ENIGMA OF ISLAMIST VIOLENCE

The CERI Series in Comparative Politics and International Studies

Series editor CHRISTOPHE JAFFRELOT

This series consists of translations of noteworthy publications in the social sciences emanating from the foremost French research centre in international studies, the Paris-based Centre d'Etudes et de Recherches Internationales (CERI), part of Sciences Po and associated with the CNRS (Centre National de la Recherche Scientifique).

The focus of the series is the transformation of politics and society by transnational and domestic factors—globalisation, migration and the postbipolar balance of power on the one hand, and ethnicity and religion on the other. States are more permeable to external influence than ever before and this phenomenon is accelerating processes of social and political change the world over. In seeking to understand and interpret these transformations, this series gives priority to social trends from below as much as the interventions of state and non-state actors.

Founded in 1952, CERI has fifty full-time fellows drawn from different disciplines conducting research on comparative political analysis, international relations, regionalism, transnational flows, political sociology, political economy and on individual states.

Amélie Blom • Laetitia Bucaille • Luis Martinez

editors

The Enigma of Islamist Violence

Translated by John Atherton, Ros Schwartz, and William Snow

Columbia University Press
New York

*In association with the Centre d'Études et de
Recherches Internationales, Paris*

Columbia University Press
Publishers Since 1893
New York

Library of Congress Cataloging-in-Publication Data

The Enigma of Islamist violence / Amélie Blom,
Laetitia Bucaille, Luis Martinez, editors.
    p. cm.
 Includes bibliographical references (p.   ) and index.
 ISBN 978-0-231-70002-3 (cloth : alk. paper)
1. Violence—Religious aspects—Islam. 2. Suicide—Religious aspects—Islam.
3. Martyrdom—Islam. 4. Suicide bombers. 5. Islam and politics. I. Blom,
A. (Amélie) II. Bucaille, Laetitia. III. Martinez, Luis, 1965– IV. Title.

 BP190.5.V56E65 2007
 297.2'7—dc22

2007020784

∞
Columbia University Press books are printed on permanent and durable acid-free paper.
This book is printed on paper with recycled content.
Printed in India
c 10 9 8 7 6 5 4 3 2 1

CONTENTS

ACKNOWLEDGEMENTS

This book grew out of a series of articles on Islamist violence (those by A. Blom, L. Bucaille, P. Larzillière and L. Martinez) originally published in the quarterly *Critique Internationale* (no. 20, "variations") by the Presses de Sciences Po, Paris, in July 2003. We would like to thank the journal's editor-in-chief, Christophe Jaffrelot, Director of the CERI, for his help at that time, as well as Rachel Bouyssou who wielded her boundless experience and sensitivity to put the articles into shape for publication. Thanks to the support of Hurst & Co. publishers, and its director, Michael Dwyer, the present collective work published in English enables us to provide a thoroughly revised and updated version of these articles for a much broader readership. It also gives us the opportunity to include a wider selection of case studies, L. du Bouchet, O. Grojean, and H. Redissi and J.E. Lane having kindly enriched the investigation we had begun with analyses pertaining to their specific fields of research. Above all, the present book offers in its introduction a survey of the state of current research on the forms of violence perpetrated by Islamist movements, as well as a comparative analysis that was absent from the French version.

Lastly, *The Enigma of Islamist Violence* could never have been possible without the patient translation work undertaken by John Atherton, Ros Schwartz, and William Snow, and even less without the careful coordination and editing of the entire manuscript by Cynthia Schoch. We extend our warm thanks to all four of them.

THE CONTRIBUTORS

AMÉLIE BLOM is an Associate researcher at the Centre de Recher-
ches Internationales de la Sorbonne (CRIS, Université Paris-I) and a
Consultant at the Centre d'Etudes et de Recherches Internationales
(CERI, Paris). She is a member of the Editorial Committee of SAMAJ
(South Asian Multidisciplinary Academic Journal - online). Her research, in Political Sociology, focuses on the Kashmir issue and on
Pakistan's politics and society. She has published (with F. Charillon)
Théories et concepts des relations internationales (Paris, Hachette, 2001) as
well as several studies and articles on Pakistan: "'Qui a le bâton, a le
buffle'. Le corporatisme économique de l'armée pakistanaise". *Ques-
tions de recherche*, n°16, décembre 2005 (http://www.ceri-sciences-
po.org/publica/question/qdr16.pdf), "The 'Multi-Vocal' State: The
Policy of Pakistan on Kashmir" in C. Jaffrelot, ed., *Pakistan. Nationalism without a Nation?*, Zed Books, 2002 and "Les partis islamistes au
Pakistan à la recherche d'un second souffle" in C. Jaffrelot, ed., *Le
Pakistan, carrefour de tensions régionales*, Bruxelles, Complexe, 2002.

LÆTITIA BUCAILLE lectures in the sociology department of the
University of Bordeaux. Since 2003, she has been a member of the
Institut Universitaire de France and associate researcher with CERI.
An Arabic speaker, she has done fieldwork in Algeria, Gaza, the West
Bank and Israel. Her work focuses mainly on the Palestinian Ter-
ritories and Israeli-Palestinian relations. She has published *Gaza: la*

violence de la paix Paris, Presses de Sciences Po, 1998, and *Growing up Palestinian: The Israeli Occupation and the Intifada Generation*, Princeton University Press, Princeton, 2004. Her current research concentrates on reconciliation issues in Sourth Africa and between France and Algeria.

LUIS MARTINEZ is a senior research fellow at CERI-Sciences-Po and lectures at the Institut d'Etudes Politiques in Paris. He was adjunct professor at SIPA, Columbia University, New York (2000-2001). He is the author of numerous articles on the Arab world and a work of reference on Algeria (*The Algerian Civil War*, London, Hurst, 2001). He is considered one of the most foremost experts on Libya (*The Libyan Paradox*, London, Hurst, 2007). At CERI he co-chairs the "New Forms of Violence Today" research group.

LUDMILA DU BOUCHET is a PhD candidate in International Relations at the University of Cambridge (United Kingdom) and a Gates Cambridge Trust scholar. Her research revolves around the relationship between state formation and international dynamics in developing countries, focusing on the reconfiguration of the Yemeni state under the impact of the US-led "global war on terror". An alumnus of the Ecole Normale Supérieure and the Institut d'Etudes Politiques (Paris, France), she is currently an associate researcher at the Centre Français d'Archéologie et de Sciences Sociales de Sana'a (Yemen), and member of the editorial committee of its *Chroniques Yéménites*. She has carried out commissioned fieldwork and consultancies for French institutions in Yemen and the West Bank. Her publications include "La politique étrangère américaine au Yémen: nouvelles pratiques sécuritaires et recomposition de la scène politique", 2004 (http://cy.revues.org/document154.html), and a case-study on Yemen in Yezid Sayigh and John Sfakianakis (eds.), *The Military and the State in the Middle East* (forthcoming).

OLIVIER GROJEAN is a PhD candidate in sociology at the Paris Ecole des Hautes Etudes en Sciences Sociales and teaches political sociology and international relations at the Université de Lille 2. His research focuses on the political commitment of the Kurds in Turkey and Europe and on sacrificial violence and the phenomena of political radicalisation. His publications include "Immigration et solidarités transnationales: l'engagement politique en exil" in Devin, Guillaume, *Les solidarités transnationales*, Paris, L'Harmattan, 2004, p. 43-57 and "Engagement militant et phénomènes de radicalisation chez les Kurdes de Turquie" (in association with Gilles Dorronsoro), *European Journal of Turkish Studies*, 2004, URL: http://www.ejts.org/document198. html.

JAN-ERIK LANE is a Swedish political scientist currently professor and head of the Political Science department at the University of Geneva.

PÉNÉLOPE LARZILLIÈRE is a researcher at the Institut de Recherche pour le Développement (IRD). She holds a PhD in sociology from the Ecole des Hautes Etudes en Sciences Sociales (EHESS). Her doctoral thesis on Palestinian youth was published in 2004 (*Etre jeune en Palestine*, Balland). Her research focuses on the relationship between Islamic and nationalist ideologies. She is currently investigating this topic by collecting social and political trajectories of activists in Jordan.

HAMADI REDISSI is professor of political science at the Faculty of Law and Political Science, University of Tunis (Tunisia). He is the author of an important reference work, *L'exception islamique*, Paris, Seuil, 2004.

FOREWORD

Islamist terrorism has been dissected *ad nauseam*, and has spawned an expanded volume of literature since the attacks of 11 September 2001. What justifies our continuing to reflect on the forms of violence perpetrated by Islamist movements? The main reason is precisely the blow of 11 September. It was so powerful that attempts to explain Islamist terrorism are still now often dismissed as attempts to defend the indefensible. This book refuses to fall into such a trap, but instead has the aim of pinpointing the conditions in which deadly Islamist violence emerges. Above all, the focus is no longer on why Muslim terrorists exist but rather on determining the reasons that lead to the decision, at a given point in time, to slide into extreme brutality.

The current debate surrounding Islamist violence remains locked in often sterile ideas of dichotomies. Are suicide attacks related to faith or to the level of socio-economic development? Is the Islamist suicide bomber a pathological case, as the psychological analyses dominating the field today portray him or her, or a clever strategist, as the geopolitical approach claims? These are the questions most often asked.

Culturalist explanations, which hold that Islamist violence is a product of a belief system (the hypothetical "line of Islamism" running from the Middle Ages to today), have cast an overbearing shadow on scholarly discourse. Such explanations inevitably slide towards belief in the aggressive nature of a religion that is described as an ethereal reality. These in fact fit within a cognitive framework that goes beyond the mere issue of violence. Islam becomes the explanation for anything and everything, from misogyny to poverty, from the lack of democracy to terrorism. The underlying assumption is actually that the problem is simply the overly central role that religion supposedly plays in the life of dominantly Muslim societies.

As for the approach through the lens of underdevelopment, it views Islamist violence as an all-encompassing fact, whereas it necessarily has multiple forms and meanings. And it is precisely these many faces of violence, in countries that are nevertheless comparable from a socio-economic standpoint, that should draw the analyst's attention. Why, for instance, have suicide attacks been so frequent in Israel and in Kashmir, but virtually non-existent in Algeria or Yemen? Macro-structural analyses of Islamist violence, whether based on the religious or the socio-economic variable, prove to be of limited use to answer this pivotal question.

Micro-sociological analyses are often just as disappointing. In their psychological version, they attempt to convince readers that there exists a typical socio-psychological profile of the terrorist, even when most empirical studies, such as those presented herein, demonstrate that the reverse is true. The strictly strategic version often confines itself to describing a terrorist organization. Such an approach has given rise to countless books on Al-Qaida as well as fastidious biographies of its major figures. But the Al-Qaida ideology is not only based on a deviant interpretation of the Muslim religion; in addition, adherence to it concerns only a minority of Islamist movements, even those that advocate violence.

Rejecting these dichotomies, the present volume takes up the problem at its roots, or, so to speak, traps the culturalist analysis in its own game, first by asking (and the question remains open): does Islam have a theory of the legitimate use of violence? (H. Redissi and J.E. Lane). And if so, how is this theory reinterpreted by the Islamists? The book then focuses primarily on the political and historical context in which radical Islamist violence takes place – a factor that is largely neglected by the current literature on Islamist terrorism. It not only studies Islamist violence in general but also specific acts of violence. This is why it gives preference, unlike most books available on the subject today, to an analysis based on case studies: the Palestinian Territories (L. Bucaille), Kashmir (A. Blom), Algeria (L. Martinez), Yemen (L. du Bouchet), Chechnya (P. Larzillière). All are the fruit of the authors' long studies in the field and/or an attentive and detailed reading of the propaganda put out by radical Islamist organizations.

By determining the individual and collective social and political motivations behind acts of violence, it becomes possible to take some distance from Islamist propaganda: in reality, a worldwide war of religion has not replaced local struggles, nor has the Umma replaced nations, nor even has the implementation of the Sharia prevented existing regimes from being overturned or nations from gaining their independence. Only the repertoires of violence have changed. How can that be explained?

Placing the descent into violence in political and temporal context of course helps to provide an answer, but only if it is connected with the study of what we call the *imaginaires* of Islamist violence, in other words the modes of subjectivization of such violence. To understand the usefulness of this approach, suffice it here to point out that violence against the state and violence against oneself necessarily derive not only from different political rationales but also from different symbolic rationales. In this respect, it is particularly helpful to compare the "Islamist" suicide attack to other "non-Islamist" modes of violence done to one's own body: the case of the Kurds is very useful for this (O. Grojean).

This book thus seeks to understand radical violence on the basis of a sociological interpretation that alone allows us to unveil the Islamists' political *imaginaire*. This imaginary construct at first glance reveals an attempt to legitimize the combat against a political authority considered as infidel, iniquitous, usurping and/or an occupying force. Categories of individuals said to stand in the way of a new Islamic social order, and/or act as accomplices of state violence, are then taken as targets. The West, perceived as arrogant, dominating, invading and/or also an accomplice of state arbitrariness, is also regularly targeted.

But a more attentive reading unveils a less obvious, and highly distinctive, universe of meaning for suicidal political violence. The quest for purity in the next world that replaces justice here on earth in which the militant no longer believes; the distress caused by the degeneracy and internal splits of a failing ethno-nationalist rebellion which encourages a shift in the struggle to a timelessness that death offers; or the paradoxical desire to assert oneself as an individual in a context marked by the group's powerlessness by carrying out an "exemplary" act of war against an enemy that is more and more fantasized – all are examples of the complex motivations behind suicide attacks that this book brings to light.

INTRODUCTION

IMAGINAIRES OF ISLAMIST VIOLENCE

Amélie Blom, Laetitia Bucaille and Luis Martinez

Since the attacks of 11 September 2001, Islamist terrorism has regularly struck its "enemies". In the Muslim world, Saudi Arabia has suffered
a recurring onslaught since 2003. There were over three hundred suicide bombings in Iraq between August 2004 and October 2005. Terrorism has now spread to Indonesia, first Bali in 2002 (when 202 were
killed in a suicide attack), then Jakarta in August 2003, then Bali again
in September 2005 (23 killed); and to Turkey (November 2003, 63
dead), Morocco (Casablanca, May 2003, 45 dead) and Tunisia (April
2002, 21 dead). In Europe Russia, Spain (11 March 2004, 191 dead)
and London (7 July 2005, 52 dead and 700 injured) have been the
targets of fatal attacks. This terrorist activity arouses new anxieties in
the public and creates the sense of an acute "threat", which is stoked
by an "apocalyptic" vision of Islam.[1] Islamist violence reawakens some
of the West's most caricatural fears of Islam. "The deep roots of Islamist fascism," one explanation goes, "lie in the very foundations of
Islamic orthodoxy, taught in the great Muslim universities the world
over, and have remained unchanged since the eleventh century. The
Koran and the Hadiths, the sources of the Sharia, explicitly proclaim
holy war …In the Koran, armed combat is called the 'path of Allah'
and the fallen mujahedin are compared to 'martyrs of the Faith'. The

1

Koran is full of surahs calling for war against the defiant Jews, Christians and polytheists."[2] The association of Islam with violence goes back a long way, but this culturalist and reductionist approach reflects Western anxiety and wariness more than it helps to comprehend the repertories of Islamist violence. In fact, the issue is obviously more complex: according to Alfred Morabia, Islamic scholars have long been divided over interpretation on the subject of *jihad*: "Jihad was a multi-faceted combat that resurfaced during different moments of Muslim history. Buried, according to some, it seemed to rise from its ashes each time the Umma went through a period of crisis or was faced with adversity."[3]

The current debate on the nature and rationality (in the sense understood by the social sciences, i.e. the suitability of the means of action to the ends) of the violence perpetrated by Islamist organizations, and in particular suicide bombings, comes down to two major questions, one related to the macro level (Islam and societies), and the other to the micro level (the terrorist actor).[4] Why, over the last thirty years, have Muslim societies produced terrorist violence? Is the violent protagonist pathological or a sophisticated strategist?

Why Islamist violence?

Four types of global factors are usually cited in order to explain the emergence of terrorist violence in the Muslim world: Islam as "sick", martyrdom as a specifically Shiite vision, terrorism as the product of socioeconomic conditions, and, lastly, terrorism as the product of state repression. At the same time, the Islamists themselves produce a discourse justifying the recourse to violence, which is worth analyzing.

The expert on Islam Bernard Lewis seeks to explain the decline of Muslim societies: "Compared with Christendom, its rival for more than a millennium, the world of Islam had become poor, weak, and ignorant. The primacy and therefore the dominance of the West were clear for all to see, invading every aspect of the Muslim's public and even—more painfully—his private life."[5] Historically, this decline can be attributed to three alleged "enemies": the Mongols, the Turks and the Europeans. And today it is the Americans who are the embodiment of this new foe, today's equivalent of the Mongols for the Iraqis combating it. Although Lewis' work paves the way for examining the question of memory in Muslim societies and their relationship to the West, the generalization implied by his argument weakens it. Furthermore, his essentialist analysis freezes Muslims in an attitude of resentment and refuses to study their modes of action and production of meaning related to such a stance.

A second factor is invoked to explain today's Islamist terrorism. For a long time, it was thought to be specific to the Shiites. The civil war in Lebanon and above all the Iranian Revolution helped foster this belief. The cult of martyrdom in Shiism led to a belief that followers of this branch of Islam had elective affinities with terrorism.[6] Conversely, the Sunni Muslims were credited with a certain degree of moderation. This perception of a "less violent" Sunni Islam originated during the period of European colonization. At that time, Islam appeared as a peaceful religion, so well had the *ulema* (religious scholars) adapted to the presence of the colonial powers. Furthermore, Islam has not always been seen by the West as an intrinsically violent religion. In the 1950s and 60s, it was the nationalist movements which represented the enemies of the West. The emergence of terrorism in Sunni Muslim societies in the 1990s gradually challenged this perception. Once again, we would argue that Islam, whether it be the Sunni or Shiite version, cannot be considered as a monolithic base that predetermines the attitudes of political actors.

Thirdly, Western anxieties stem from the idea that these states produce "dangerous societies" and are a fertile breeding ground for the terrorist organization Al-Qaida. The United Nations report on *Human Development in the Arab World* (2002), written by Arab experts, raised new concerns about the stability of the international system. The authors show that the population of the Arab world, estimated at

280 million in 2000, will reach approximately 480 million by 2020. This population growth is taking place in an economic context fraught with political consequences. Overall, the economies of the Arab countries remain unproductive, and, at the present rate, it will take 120 years for incomes simply to double! Despite their petrodollars, the economic importance of the Arab states has had little impact on the world. For example, in 1999, the Arab countries' GDP of $530 billion was not even equal to Spain's $595 billion. The Arab world thus remains hindered by structural disadvantages – low incomes, low investment, illiteracy, the condition of women etc. – which foment social instability and violence. This is all the more worrying as young people in Arab societies cannot imagine that their living conditions will improve, owing to the political obstacles inherent in authoritarian regimes. Taking economic and social conditions into account may produce objective data on the state of societies, but this obviously does not help to explain ideological outputs and the descent into violence.

François Burgat stresses that it is indeed state authoritarianism and repression that produce Islamist violence.[7] He re-situates the use of violence by Islamist groups in the context of the brutal and enduring domination of the dictatorial regimes of various Arab countries. In Burgat's view, Islamist violence is a reaction to state violence; he points out that some of these movements abandoned the attempt to act within the confines of legality only after recognizing the failure of their strategy. His theory also applies to the international arena: military occupations by superpowers smacking of colonization, or Western governments' support for detested authoritarian leaders of southern countries, exacerbate the population's resentment and exasperation. Initially Islamist groups take on these frustrations, around which they produce a system of meanings; and then, at a later stage, they organize reprisals against the "iniquitous" West.

Burgat's approach has the merit of putting the various Islamist movements' slide into violence back into perspective, comparing it to another type of brutality, that of the state. However, it makes it even harder to understand the attacks which do not affect leaders or the state apparatus, but civilian targets that have nothing to do with the confrontation between the political powers and their opponents. If the political regime is emphasized as the prime factor in Islamist violence, it is also tempting to consider that democratization and good governance would be the cure-all for eradicating the terrorist threat in the Arab and Muslim states. This is why the present "war on terror" goes hand in hand with measures aimed at forcing the regimes of Muslim states to reform, either by force or as a result of diplomatic and economic pressure. Thus Saudi Arabia, Kuwait and Syria are in a position where they are forced to liberalize their regimes and Pakistan to reform its school system (restricting the freedom of the *madrasas*, rewriting textbooks, etc.). But the challenge lies elsewhere: for the Bush administration, anti-Americanism and anti-Zionism are above all the result of propaganda by authoritarian Arab states;[8] so, once freed from servitude and integrated into democratic regimes, Muslim societies will no longer have any reason to share hatred of the USA.[9]

The war in Iraq thus became the symbol of this policy of promoting democracy, through the use of force if necessary.[10] It was a question of "liberating" societies subject to dictatorial regimes in order to encourage the development of new values: democracy, freedom and liberalism. This has sparked a debate in the Arab world: is democracy the best response to Islamist terrorism?

In opposition to these different analyses — from the media, the academic world and the political world — are interpretations of the violence by the Islamic authorities and Muslim theologians themselves, which attest to the difficulties in justifying it from a religious point of view. Indeed, Islamist terrorism, and more precisely the use of suicide bombings as a weapon, represents a new departure in the history of Islam. In deliberately seeking death, the "terrorist" certainly causes his suicide. However, in Islam suicide is condemned, and there are many Muslim theologians who do not consider it as an act of martyrdom.

For Imam Muhammad Nasirudin Al-Albani, "All the suicide missions of our time are unpunished acts which should be considered as forbidden [haram]. The suicide missions may count among the actions that lead the perpetrator into the eternal flames or place him among those who will not burn in the eternal flames ...But to see these suicide missions as a means drawing closer to Allah (a praiseworthy act of worship) by killing oneself today for one's land or one's country, to that we say no! These suicide missions are not Islamic!"[11]

This rejection of suicide bombings is part of a traditional interpretation of violence in Islam. Over the centuries, theologians have drawn up very precise rules on the conditions for waging jihad, and until now, there was no place for suicide bombing. First of all because deliberate death is associated with suicide and not with seeking to defend Islam; suicide is indeed a sin in Islam, leading to eternal punishment. Secondly because there is a clear distinction between fighting and non-fighting victims. For the theologian Ibn Taymiyya (1263-1328), "Those who, like women, children, priests, the elderly, the blind and the disabled, etc. cannot be considered as 'resistance fighters' or 'fighters', will not be killed, according to the generally accepted view, unless they have effectively fought only those whom we fight, for we want the religion of God to triumph."[12] For the Grand Mufti of Saudi Arabia, Sheikh Al Aziz Bin Abdallah, acts of self-destruction are more akin to suicide than martyrdom: "I do not know of any provision in religious law regarding the act of killing oneself amid one's enemies...That is not part of the jihad ... Even though the Koran authorises and even demands the killing of our enemies, it must be done in a way that complies with the Sharia."[13]

The suicide bombings that claim victims are however justified by some theologians such as Al Qaradawi on the pretext that "In Israel, every Jewish citizen, male and female, does military service, and is therefore a potential soldier".[14] Al Qaradawi however points out that rather than the suicide bombing, it is the motivation behind it that confers status of martyr: "Any Muslim who attests that there is no other God but God and that Muhammad is the Prophet, who is not guilty of apostasy (in mocking an element of the faith, in refusing an obligation, in considering a peremptory ban legitimate or scorning a consensual point of the Sharia) – if he is killed in the battle between Muslims and the infidel Jews – is a martyr Muslim in his own right. He enjoys all the provisions befitting martyrs: he is neither washed nor wrapped in a shroud and is buried in the clothes he was wearing when killed so that the bloodstains and wounds testify in his favour on the Day of Resurrection. As for the question of knowing whether his struggle and his bloody death are on the Path of God (*Sabil Allah*) or not, it depends on his intentions, his motives and purpose, which in Islam are the criteria for evaluating all actions...The Struggle (*Jihad*) in Islam is not a material act. It is rather an act of self-sacrifice and one of the greatest acts of worship that brings the faithful close to God. It is for this reason that approval of this act of worship depends on a total abnegation of intentions in favour of God, as well as on the purification of the heart of all material motives such as the quest for renown, heroic pride or nationalist fanaticism."[15]

So to achieve this status, the potential suicide bomber faces two challenges: to prove that the reasons motivating his attack are pure, and to prove that through this act, he is working solely to defend Islam. Suicide is indeed a sin in Islam, leading to eternal punishment. The suicide bombers of 11 September 2001 raise a thorny theological problem: are they terrorists or martyrs? If the subjective intention of the author of the attack becomes the criterion for legitimating his act, this leaves almost total latitude for interpretation, and the problem shifts without being solved: who is responsible for recognising the would-be martyrs' purity of intent? It is easier to justify this status through the classic defence of Islam. Islamist organizations justify their use of violence by their desire to set themselves up as defenders of the Muslim community under attack. From the Palestinian Territories to Chechnya, from Iraq to Kashmir, Islamist organizations condemn the failure of the leaders of the Arab and Muslim states to come to the aid of their co-religionists. The inability of the Arab and Muslim regimes to protect a Muslim community justifies the *jihad* against the infidel rulers attacking it: the Russians in Afghanistan and Chechnya, the Israelis in the Palestinian Territories, the Indians in Kashmir, and the Americans in Iraq. From this point of view, the "new martyrs" are those who have the courage to sacrifice themselves to defend a Muslim community. But this community is simply reinvented. "This imaginary *umma* can take the form of historical paradigms (the Ottoman empire), political myths (the caliphate) or the categories of traditional Islam (*dar ul harb, dar ul islam* – country of war, country of Islam) but blurred since [...] this no longer corresponds to a territory" as Olivier Roy points out.[16]

The terrorist: strategist or pathogenic actor?

To portray Islamist activists who perpetrate acts of violence or terrorism as "Allah's madmen" hardly helps further our understanding of the phenomenon. As irrational as they may initially seem to us, analysis of their discourse, their agenda and their methods reveal their ability to calculate and develop strategies and to take advantage of their enemy's weaknesses. This capacity for anticipating and producing modes of action places Islamist terrorists within the sphere of rational violent action.[17] Three types of approach provide clues as to what makes the protagonists turn to violence. We will outline in turn what the strategic, psychological and sociological approaches offer as keys to understanding the phenomenon.

A strategic analysis presents terrorism as a means that weak actors use to compensate for the growing imbalance of power on the international stage. This phenomenon is part of a change in the traditional frameworks of the post-Westphalian model, where non-state actors, including diasporas and transnational networks, are increasingly asserting themselves and challenging the states' prerogatives. Robert Pape, for instance, draws an analogy between terrorism and methods of economic or military coercion resorted to by the international community and individual states.[18] In taking a particularly close look at the rising phenomenon of suicide bombings, Pape rejects explanations couched in culturalist or psychological terms. On the one hand, he demonstrates that although the Arab and Muslim world is the focus of attention today, the most prolific perpetrators of suicide bombings are to be found among the Liberation Tigers of Tamil Eelam (LTTE) in Sri Lanka, who are a Hindu and Marxist organization. On the other hand, he shows that it is impossible to draw up a psychological and social profile of the suicide bomber whose gender, level of education, family situation and socio-economic milieu vary. For Pape acts of terrorism, and particularly suicide bombings, obey a strategic logic aimed at forcing liberal democracies to make territorial concessions and to apply the principle of self-determination.[19] In his view, the increase in suicide bombings results from the terrorists' perception that this strategy pays off because the states targeted have often given in. Pape emphasizes however that it is hard to evaluate the terrorists' "success", for in actual fact a government's response depends on a number of factors. Furthermore, it is highly unlikely that states would concede vital issues concerning security or their national wealth under the pressure of terrorist acts, however forceful.

In reality, it seems that the most effective outcome of terrorist activity is not so much a shift in the balance of political or territorial power as the impact on the society which is the butt of the attacks. In fact, terrorist strategy works if it achieves its own purpose, which is to terrorize the target population or group. Thus it wins a definitive battle when it succeeds in destroying a society's conviction that it is immune from the danger of violent death and instils instead a sense of fear and insecurity. The impact of terrorism is therefore measured not so much by the number of human losses it inflicts but by the response it arouses in the target population. Pape subscribes to this analysis and states that suicide bombings are more likely to spread a feeling of vulnerability within a society insofar as the principle behind them exceeds the traditional norms of violence.

Strategic analysis has the merit of putting Islamist violence and regional or international power struggles into perspective, but is not sufficient to take account of all the social and historical processes underpinning these acts. It also fails to explain what pushes an individual to turn to violent action.

Psychological studies have the advantage of tackling the phenomenon of Islamist violence by looking closely at those involved. Some Islamist groups operate like sects, and it is important to highlight the pressures exerted on the individual and the atmosphere that prevails once they have joined. Psychology sheds a useful light on group dynamics, the identification and alienation processes, the way a leader can mesmerize his recruits and subject them to his will, and the process of breaking away and turning inwards observed in some groups. Furthermore, analysis of the sense of frustration and, above all, humiliation that can be felt by individuals is very enlightening in explaining forms of commitment and recourse to violent action.[20]

Nevertheless, psychological analysis alone can be insufficient if it is not combined with other approaches. If it is divorced from the cultural, historical, social and political context surrounding individuals, it risks reducing the members of radical Islamist groups to "unbalanced", "frustrated" individuals, megalomaniacs spurred to the worst extremes by poverty and ignorance. That is the somewhat heuristic current hypothesis of the fanatical terrorist manipulated by cynical leaders. However, the psychologist Scott Atran concludes that the "suicide bombers" have no observable "pathology", and that their level of education and economic well-being is comparable to that of the majority of the population in the countries where they live.[21] To understand why individuals who display no particular pathology volunteer for suicide missions, we need in fact to look at the protagonists' representations and their *imaginaire*, which take on a psychological but also a political dimension: in the context of the Middle East, the collective sense of a historic injustice,[22] of political dependency, and the vague feeling of being humiliated by the superpowers and their allies would all be explanatory factors. These feelings are unquestionably a factor, and the following chapters attempt to put them into perspective. However, it could be claimed that these are shared by a great many Palestinians, Chechens or Kashmiris who are not prepared to blow themselves up in order to eliminate those they hold responsible for their frustration. Similarly, it is also vital to stress that the sense of historic injustice or humiliation shared by many formerly colonized societies or societies under attack has not led to a manifestation of radical or terrorist violence.

And then, psychological analysis comes up against a twofold methodological stumbling block. Solitude, perceived as a main component of the militant's psychic life, can just as well be an utterly banal feeling for a prisoner or activist who has broken away from his native society. Then, and without straying into culturalism, ethno-psychoanalysis is there to remind us that feelings of solitude, abandonment, humiliation and despair are certainly universal, but the situations that inspire them vary considerably according to the nature of people's expectations: in other words, according to the universe of meaning, the nature of social control and the dominant hierarchical structures specific to each society.

The socio-political approach also seeks to understand the reasoning behind the violence by focusing on the protagonists. It explores the different modes of operation of the groups of actors and their position within a political relationship, as well as their social roots. It has the virtue of re-establishing the full importance of the political variable. Different authors have helped build a sociological portrait of the Islamists who turn to violent action. Nevertheless, this type of study comes up against the limits of its feasibility: it is, for example, hard to meet people who are planning to become suicide bombers or to plant bombs. One exception is the recording of Khaled Kelkal's testimony by a German sociologist, Dietmar Loch.[23] This interview is highly instructive: it enables us to situate the activist's family background, follow his initially promising school career and his going off the rails when, at his new secondary school, he finds himself in a bourgeois milieu of French origin. And then, we learn that he turns to delinquency, resulting in imprisonment and his discovery of Islam in jail. This document enables us to retrace the story of a bomber. By analyzing the various profiles and trajectories of 172 participants in the Salafist *jihad*, Marc Sageman also seeks to identify the reasons why individuals join a terrorist organization.[24] His research demonstrates the importance of social bonds within networks and ties of friendship and loyalty among groups that predated any ideological and activist commitment. Sageman dispels a cliché depicting cynical leaders indoctrinating vulnerable youths by showing that recruitment into organizations promoting *jihad* occurs by a "bottom-up process" in which youths volunteer of their own free will. His approach still does not enable us to grasp the reasons why individuals decide to embrace radical violence.

From the sociological standpoint, the main driving force for suicide bombing is a context of impotence and permanent insecurity.[25] Political murder and taking one's own life are, then, a reversal of domination, an act that brings "empowerment" (a central notion which means, in this context, "giving oneself the power"), certainty and self-respect. It could be objected that this functionalist interpretation (what benefit does suicide bombing bring the would-be bomber?) is biased by the very nature of the study, which encourages the interviewee to make his act sound heroic and to aggrandize himself in denouncing the crimes of others. Yet this method has the great virtue of allowing those to speak who, generally, are only allowed to do so arbitrarily.

Gilles Kepel, meanwhile, sheds an interesting light on Islamist violence by stressing the power struggle that goes on within Islamist movements, when they are part of the opposition.[26] The interests of the different social groups that comprise it are divergent and the choice of strategy to adopt depends on the importance of each one. So there is a likelihood of switching to extreme violence when there is a split between the pious bourgeoisie – often anxious to preserve its peace of mind and therefore to prefer a *modus vivendi* with the ruling powers – and deprived urban youth. This latter group is more ready to risk the little it has in a confrontation with the state. Supported by an Islamist intelligentsia, it accelerates and deepens the rift with the bourgeois element and turns to *jihad*.

The strength of the sociologist Farhad Khosrokhavar's analysis comes from his ability to achieve a balance lacking in so many approaches: he makes the link between expectations, both individual and of various kinds, as well as the deadly action that they lead to, and a collective, social and political mode of action. He looks particularly closely at the forms of Islamist mobilization that lead to the experience of "martyrdom".[27] The global approach that aims to grasp the protagonists' motivations and thought systems, to penetrate their subjectivity, is particularly edifying. The figure of the "martyropath", a term coined by Khosrokhavar, in the Iranian case is characterized by despair, guilt and personal failure to fully enter the modern world. When he becomes aware that the Islamist utopia cannot be salvaged, he is not only overwhelmed, but also stopped in his progress towards the promised modernity. So the choice to die as a "martyr" aims to reassure him of his own individuality and is the only possible route to achieve this. The failure of the Iranian revolution and its egalitarian utopia, the social and psychic dislocation resulting from the shattering of communities and the traditional family model, and the forced renegotiation of the relationship to modernity and Western domination are equally important factors which make the fascination with death understandable.

Khosrokhavar has also tried to grasp the motivations of the Al-Qaida "neo-martyrs", Muslims chiefly living in and assimilated into Western countries. He suggests that their extreme violence has its roots in the profound hatred they appear to have developed for the West. The sociologist deciphers different forms of humiliation that authors of suicide bombings might have suffered. The first is that felt by an individual member of an immigrant community in a European or American country; the second is felt vicariously when watching media reports of the spectacle of the war in Bosnia or clashes in the Palestinian Territories; and lastly, immersion within a Western society might create a sense of being tainted. Joining a movement that formalizes and organizes the struggle against the "arrogant" West is, it is suggested, a means of restoring lost dignity.

Islamist violence: An alternative approach

Both the macro-structural analysis of Islamist violence, whether it retains the religious or the socioeconomic variable, and the micro-analysis focused on a terrorist actor with strictly strategic or pathogenic orientations prove of limited use for a number of reasons. On the one hand, they view Islamist violence as a monolithic phenomenon, when of course it is many-sided and polysemous. On the other hand, the political and historical context in which this violence occurs is clearly neglected. And lastly, analysts often find it easier to yield to the temptation to take Islamist propaganda literally (global religious war as a substitute for local struggles, the Umma for nations, and the application of the Sharia for the overthrow of existing regimes or independence) rather than to undertake a sociological interpretation. Such an interpretation is certainly difficult, but has the immeasurable merit of taking into account the protagonists' political *imaginaire* of violence, and therefore making the transition to radical violence intelligible.

The present work, which develops the sociological and anthropological intuitions of research such as Farhad Khosrokhavar's, thus chooses to study individual local acts of violence. Situated in time and space, these are perpetrated by Islamist organizations, and/or individuals claiming an affinity with these organizations (when isolated acts are carried out, as in the Palestinian Territories), with political motivations and multiple subjectivities. That is why we have opted for an analysis of Islamist violence based on case studies of activists located in the Palestinian Territories, Kashmir, Chechnya, Algeria and Yemen.

However, far be it from our intentions to confine ourselves merely to establishing the potentially unlimited variety of forms of violence, militant objectives and representations. It goes without saying that these vary according to particular local or national situations. But we aim to identify the conditions for the emergence of Islamist violence. It is no longer a question of "Why are there suicidal Muslim terrorists?" but of determining the reasons that lead to their choosing, at a particular moment, to turn towards extreme brutality. In order to do this, we have opted for three different types of analysis: the repertoires of collective action[28] used by Islamist militants, a political and temporal contextualization of the transition to violence, and the modes of subjectivization of this violence.

In discussing Islamist violence we examine essentially an attempt to legitimize struggle against a political power considered as infidel, iniquitous and a usurper, and/or as an occupying force,[29] and against categories of people designated as disrupters of the Islamic social order and/or accomplices of state violence;[30] also against the West, perceived as arrogant, dominating, an invader and/or an accomplice to the arbitrariness of the state. Since the 1970s, this violence has been expressed in a number of different forms and to very different degrees (bombings and ambushes in the early days of the Chechen civil war, guerrilla techniques employed by the Palestinian Intifada and by the Kashmiri jihadists, hostage-taking in Yemen, collective massacres in Algeria, suicide bombings, etc.). It must be stressed that there is no form of violence that is the exclusive prerogative of the Islamist movements. On the contrary, Olivier Grojean demonstrates clearly in his article that suicide bombing, for example, is consistent with violence against the self used for political ends by a number of non-Islamist groups, notably the Marxist Kurdish group, the PKK.

Moreover, the awkward question of attributing responsibility for such acts of violence needs to be addressed. While responsibility for most of them is claimed by Islamist organizations, we are forced to recognize, without resorting to some conspiracy theory, that in some instances it is difficult to identify those responsible, or even to exclude the involvement of the state security services, in massacres of civilians in Algeria or suicide bombings in India, for example.[31] And finally, it is important to distinguish between violence carried out principally - although never exclusively - against the representatives of the state (security services, government departments etc.) and/or one-off acts against isolated individuals, as in Kashmir for example, and violence aimed collectively and regularly at civilians, as happens in the Palestinian Territories. We reserve the term "terrorism" only for the latter type of violence.

These caveats having been stated, we can still question the primacy given by Islamist movements in recent years to particular repertoires of action. Hostage-taking, used by Lebanese militias under the more or less firm control of foreign powers during the 1980s, and in Yemen, made its appearance in Pakistan with the murder of the journalist Daniel Pearl in February 2002, then in Iraq from 2003 on. In the latter two cases, it is characterized by morbid media interest, via the internet or video cassettes deliberately designed to frighten Western audiences. Suicide bombings, common in Lebanon in the 1980s, have become increasingly prevalent in Israel since 1994, appeared in Kashmir in 2000, and have spread to Chechnya and Russia and, since 2001, to the Western world.

As weapons of the weak against the strong, hostage-taking and suicide bombings have an indisputable strategic effectiveness. The political and symbolic effectiveness of this mode of action lies, indeed, in the feeling of total insecurity it creates. Governments seem utterly at a loss when it comes to anticipating and preventing such actions. It could be said that if the main change brought by guerrilla war compared with conventional war was the shift from the capturing of territorial positions to gaining a hold over a people and commanding them to pledge support for the rebels, the effect of suicide bombings, and to a lesser extent hostage-taking, is indeed to create a "community of insecurity". The dramatic art of cruelty, beyond the moral indignation it arouses, is far from being anecdotal. Indeed, in addition to the strategic intention, these repertoires of action, and the over-intervention they generate, have a complex meaning. What is at work here is the concretization of a contrast between the "impurity" of the victim and the "purity" of the activist's cause. We feel this indicates not only a mutation in the *imaginaires* of violence but also a redefinition of the relationship to the Other made by contemporary Islamist movements.

However - and let us establish this from the outset - although a reading of the chapters in this book will help illuminate the question, the notion of suicide bombings is itself not entirely straightforward. First of all, suicide bombings are neither described nor perceived as such by those who perpetrate them, who prefer the term of "*fedayeen* actions" (in Pakistan/Kashmir) or "military operations" (in the Palestinian Territories). And then, "suicide bombing" is a difficult subject to pin down: attempts at a definition[32] must not mask multiple realities. Up to what point is the suicide process assumed? Is an individual who enters a military barracks, shooting on sight soldiers whose return fire guarantees his almost certain death (as is frequent in Kashmir) comparable to someone who stuffs his belt with explosives before blowing himself up in a bus alongside his victims (the most common occurrence in the Palestinian Territories)? The former, who is chiefly targeting the security forces, is different from the latter, who deliberately seeks to injure civilian targets. Although the two merit separate analyses, the fact that they both assume their wish to die as a *shahid* (martyr) justifies their being considered as one and the same phenomenon: suicidal violence whose main characteristic is, precisely, to "erode the boundary between the agent and the target".[33]

In addition to the need for a very precise study of the repertoires of action used, we consider that the violent acts carried out in the name of Islam are wholly unintelligible if they are not re-situated within the long history of political protest from which they derive. In other words, Islamist violence is a political rather than a religious phenomenon. Why the preference for one repertoire of collective action over another? Can this choice be explained by comparable political, social, organizational, even individual situations? As Islamist violence has spread around the globe, some are tempted to make a connection between all the attacks claiming political and religious legitimacy. Intellectually, there is some reason to consider the phenomenon in its entirety: the interaction between the local and the global can indeed operate when the international "*jihad*" against the West becomes a means of redeployment for Islamists who consider that confrontation with their own regime is ineffective and too costly in terms of repression.[34]

However, it seems essential to us to refocus our attention on the local, which is the only possible way of grasping the specific issues confronting the protagonists of violence and understanding the structures of political opportunities that characterize their strategic choices. These structures reveal complex situations: dubious intimacy with the state or the political authorities (Pakistan, Yemen, Islamist organizations vis-à-vis the Palestinian Authority), violence against the state prevailing over violence against the self, drawing on local registers (Algeria), violence against the state drawing on exogenous registers (Chechnya), etc. It is therefore crucial to resist the temptation to associate all Islamists who resort to a form of violence with the Al-Qaida organization. Ludmila du Bouchet, writing about Yemen, demonstrates the total inadequacy of this simplification as well as its concrete implications for the anti-terrorist struggle. Instead of envisaging Islamist violence as a "transnational and deterritorialized" phenomenon, it is therefore preferable to start from local situations and then see how these are related to the international context. This relation can be in the form of a breakaway, as shown by the enrolment of young Algerians in international Islamist networks that are at odds with the sense of violence in the local "war culture". Interaction with the international level can also take the form of borrowing, as in the spread and imitation of the action repertoire in Chechnya; or interpretation of the positions of the international community, a forceful example being the cruelly felt world indifference in the Palestinian case; or displacement (of an originally national struggle abroad, as in the case of the Madrid bombings); or extension of a conflict, as in the subcontracting of war by a state, Pakistan, in the irredentist conflict over Kashmir; or reactions to the instrumentalization of international agendas by the state, particularly in the war on terror in Yemen.

When Islamist violence is placed back in context, an additional dimension emerges which also seems crucial to us: the temporality of this violence. Indeed the political and media importance that an organization like Al-Qaida has gained[35] must not disguise the fact that in a number of local conflicts - the Palestinian Territories, Kashmir, Chechnya -, the political Islamist organizations only recently switched to suicide bombing tactics. Furthermore, the influence of international jihadism and/or its entry into the local arena (Chechen Wahhabism and Pakistani jihadists operating in Kashmir) must not blind us to an initial fact: in both these cases, as in the Palestinian Territories, the motivations of the actors are above all nationalist. In addition, we note that, very often, the switch to forms of radical violence, and in particular to suicide bombing, comes as if to seal the failure of a territory's liberation struggle against a controlling force or occupation perceived as illegitimate. This switch makes it possible, temporarily, to reverse a position of structural inferiority both politically and militarily. Suicidal political violence is not the denial of a visible and painful situation of failure but its metamorphosis into a sort of victory, for it is limitless.[36] Terrorism is indeed the culmination of a political process and not its beginning.

Political understanding of Islamist violence, then, implies referring to the principles of supply and demand. Firstly, the strategies of the organizers who direct the bombings must be examined. Their choice is the outcome of a political calculation, an evaluation of the balance of power and the risks of struggle. Then it is important to understand the organizational dynamics which in fact vary enormously: there can be a firmly rooted organization, both political and charitable, switching to armed action (the Palestinian Hamas); an ideologically disoriented organization using the "Al-Qaida" label as a resource to gain legitimacy (the Algerian GSPC); armed groups formed during the first Afghanistan war going over to the cause of another border *jihad* but with a weak social base (jihadist organizations active in Kashmir); etc. And lastly, the rationality of violent organizations needs to be analyzed in the light of the struggles splitting the militant space itself: political rivalry between Hamas and Al Fatah in the Palestinian Territories, ideological disputes between Wahhabi organizations and Sufi brotherhoods in Chechnya, sectarian religious antagonism between Pakistani jihadist organizations trying to convert their recruits to their schools of thought, etc.

This organizational "supply" responds to a "demand", that of the recruits, who sometimes exceed it (in the case of the Palestinian Territories) - which it controls, or even creates . The methods of indoctrination (for example the Pakistani jihadist organizations) and of incorporation into a network (the Palestinian Territories), but also the professionalization of the activists (in the case of Kurdish Marxist militants), are all factors that help explain the disposition towards physical self-annihilation in the name of a political cause. Nevertheless, the Islamist organizations' capacity for recruiting volunteers for violent actions also depends on the relationship between the Islamist groups and the political community in whose name they are fighting. The accommodation of a local or national struggle into a religious eschatology, *jihad*, is a discursive resource which makes it possible to win the approval of one's own political community, even to be able to count on the wider support of the global Muslim community. However, this approval is far from being total, as is demonstrated by the difficulty the international jihadists have had in establishing themselves in Chechnya.

As in the past, the support of the political community varies considerably from one situation to another, and disapproval and rejection can be vehement. This can trigger an inversion process, according to Michel Wieviorka's inversion theory: the terrorist group distances itself from "concrete social relations, to which the activist only refers in mythic or ideological terms".[37] This is a key factor in explaining the switch to violence; it can also be exacerbated as the result of the growing isolation of the group responsible for the violence within its community. This process of breaking loose from social ties, leading to increased radicalization, is observable in both Kashmir and Chechnya.

If the political substance of the conflict helps us gain some insight into the progressive radicalization of the Islamist organizations, there is a second variable that we feel is absolutely crucial in furthering our understanding of the protagonists' motivation: the methods of subjectivization of violence. Here it is a question of entering the activists' political *imaginaire* to grasp the meaning they are attempting to produce by reinventing political violence. According to J.-F. Bayart, "The *imaginaire* is first of all an interaction, since 'an image' is merely another relationship: that is, an interaction between the past, the present and a projected future, but also an interaction between social actors or between societies, whose relations are filtered by their respective 'imagining consciousness'."[38] There is a lot to be learned from this political *imaginaire*, reworked according to the contexts and historicity of local struggles. First of all, as Redissi and Lane show, the link between sanctification of the struggle in the name of the *jihad* and the instigation of a strategy attempting to apply this *jihad* here and now is far from linear or obvious. In fact it requires transmutation of the exegesis of the Koran into a modernity which is naturally foreign to it, by reason of the division of the world into states. Then, this subjectivization of violence results in repertoires of action that differ according to the historical models from which the Islamists take their inspiration. Thus in Algeria, the massacres committed by the GIA draw on the types of violence associated over many years with colonization and then decolonization. Similarly, in Chechnya, the activists draw on the semantic register of the nineteenth-century Caucasian wars. And lastly, in Pakistan, the figure of the martyr fighting in Kashmir is linked to official Islamic nationalism, Islamist and praetorian, which was built up between the 1960s and 1980s.

Through analysis of the *imaginaires* of violence of the Islamist movements, the religious justification for the suicide bombings and the way it is received can now be read differently. Indeed, the *jihad* has to be seen as a discursive resource with multiple aims: to legitimize the political homicide of an infidel and an apostate figure which the Islamists extend to a growing number of categories of society, as is emphasized by Redissi and Lane; the acquisition of spoils which the prebendary *jihad* then sanctifies, or to break the political isolation by inventing a transnational brotherhood of fighters of the faith, as Martinez demonstrates with regard to the Algerian situation; also to put an end to individual solitude by inventing a warrior camaraderie and fighting against the impurity of the political space, even against the internal evils which damage the movement's credibility and the purity of its commitment, as Blom describes in relation to the Pakistani and Kashmiri recruits; to re-establish the honour of the community and the prestige of the loser, and also affirm the superiority of the organization through the strength of its members' conviction, as Bucaille's analysis of the Palestinian movement illustrates; or again, to challenge patriarchal authority by referring to a higher power and glorifying a national struggle through making it part of a religious eschatology, as described by Larzillière in the Chechen case.

Although the motivations for each situation have specific significance, in three different situations – the Palestinian Territories, Kashmir and Chechnya – it is striking to note how in each case two factors coincide: the emergence of an increasingly blatant Puritanism and the contradictions in which nationalist and then Islamic guerrilla struggles become mired. The Islamic register thus culminates in a self-destructive violence, depending on whether attempts at redemption have emerged after years of fruitless struggle (as with the Palestinian Territories, Kashmir, Chechnya) or, on the contrary, the fighter still believes in the possibility of changing the political order here on earth (as with Algeria). Here appears a particularly heuristic dialogue partnership between two political figures, the "pure" and the "righteous", each leading to specific registers of violence.

Furthermore, the comparison helps elucidate another equally important component, linking all the martyr phenomena, in the Palestinian Territories, Kashmir, Chechnya, even Turkish Kurdistan: the affirmation of a social identity. Indeed, even if the motivations of future suicide bombers stem from a variety of rationales, it appears that, in all cases, this type of commitment, which involves killing oneself and others, paradoxically reveals itself to be a means of affirming the self. The figures – in the sociological sense of the word – of the exemplary hero, the activist loyal to his cause to the death, the all-powerful arbiter imposing his truth on one and all against all odds, the avenger of a collective humiliation and/or the loss of a loved one, the *mujahid* paying the price of his own death for the Islamization of his family entourage, the martyr who has purified himself from all stains in a redemptive death, can effectively be analyzed as different paths towards what Hamit Bozarslan calls the emergence of a positive subject.[39] Unable to fit his collective political objective into a constructive process, unable too to envisage the accomplishment of his personal project in an environment perceived as being hopeless, the activist, in annihilating himself, displaces his fulfilment as an active agent of change to a perpetual afterlife.

We have given a great deal of consideration to empirical studies based on surveys on the ground, as a choice of method as much as a working hypothesis; Islamist violence cannot be interpreted *in abstracto*. The testimonies of "martyrs" and the pamphlets or videos of the Islamist organizations only effectively reveal their meaning when seen in the light of what is learned from observation in the field. Furthermore, as we have emphasized, escalation towards increasingly violent forms of action becomes clearer in the light of an evaluation of the way they are received in society. But these empirical studies are inevitably incomplete. This is explained by the sensitivity of the political context, and the difficulty in gaining access to some sources and some regions. We are aware that only a microsociology of the would-be martyrs, based on a significant number of one-on-one interviews, exploring their individual development in the light of a precise knowledge of their private lives but also of their family, social and political environments, would enable us to draw firm conclusions. Our work should therefore be read more as possible avenues of research, which we hope are helpful, rather than definitive statements. However, interviews with relatives, martyrs' written testimonies and propagandist literature remain very valuable stopgaps.

The first chapter discusses Islamist violence in a historical light. Pinpointing the continuities and breaks in relation to the Islamic scriptures represented by the Islamists' relationship to violence is a crucial starting point for any discussion on terrorism (Hamadi Redissi and Jan-Erik Lane). The following three chapters analyze suicide bombings, or more generally the phenomenon of "martyrdom", in three specific situations which are all, and this is of course no coincidence, nationalist struggles: the Palestinian Territories (Laetitia Bucaille), Kashmir (Amélie Blom) and Chechnya (Pénélope Larzillière). Olivier Grojean's chapter sheds new light on this extreme form of violence against the self – suicide bombing – by examining it from the perspective of a broader issue: that of the political signification of violence against one's own body. And that is precisely the interest of the cases of Algeria (Luis Martinez) and Yemen (Ludmila du Bouchet), developed in the two remaining chapters of the book, focusing on the relationship between the Islamist organizations and the state. The first case shows that the failure of Islamist mobilization to achieve its political objectives does not necessarily lead to deadly violence. The second stresses that the variety of forms of Islamist violence depends as much on the shifting interpenetrations between the state and the Islamists as on the impact of the "war on terror " itself.

1

DOES ISLAM PROVIDE A THEORY OF VIOLENCE?

Hamadi Redissi and Jan-Erik Lane

The events of 11 September 2001 inevitably raise the question of the place of violence in Islam and the Arab-Muslim world. It is essential to return to original sources in order to understand our conception of this violence and compare the terrorists' use of terror with the traditional theories of the Koran. In the pages that follow we will analyze three types of logic that justify violence as the means to an end. One can, in normative terms, cast doubt on the idea of rationalizing violence. Yet violence is considered from a teleological point of view as a continuation by different means of Islam's policy of domination. As will be seen, however, it is difficult to fit terrorism into this logic. Before presenting the three "rationalities" we shall first provide background so as better to understand the status of violence in Islam.

The division of the world according to Islam

The Sharia does not, strictly speaking, deal with matters of international law. But it is possible to extract from the Sharia a certain number of principles that apply to international bodies and rules of humanitarian law. Islam is a formal, universal religion. God is one, but men live separately in tribes and nations. The Muslim religion, in that it considers itself to be the most recent, has devised a doctrine that divides the universe into three worlds. This division is not solidly anchored in the text of the Koran, but is an integral part of Muslim legal and political doctrine.

The first world is the world, or house, of Islam (*dar al-Islam*). Here it is not a question of geographical territory, but of a religious sphere *intra muros*. It is the world in which Islamic law or the Sharia reigns supreme, applied throughout and respected by all. This world is considered a haven of peace, security and justice. It includes the Muslims themselves, the subjugated minorities that have accepted protection, and those foreigners who are passing through. The second world or house is the world of war (*dar al-harb*). It is a hostile world, *extra muros*, in which non-Islamic law is applied or in which Muslims cannot practice their religion; it is also a world of insecurity and injustice. It can be distant from the land of Islam or adjacent to it. The third world is the world of reconciliation or alliance known as *dar solh*. It is a neutral territory, which to be sure does not apply Muslim law, but is a region with which Islam is at peace. Such was the case of Ethiopia, of Nubia (part of Egypt) and Cyprus.

In contemporary society, however, changes have come about. We can conceive a fourth world unforeseen by the Sharia. Arab states (22 in number) and Islamic states (57 if the Arab states are included in the total) are today independent sovereign states. As we have seen, the domestic laws by which they are governed have eliminated the distinction between the infidels and the People of the Book. The constitutions of these states recognize freedom of thought and the People of the Book are no longer obliged to pay a head tax. In addition, these states are members of the United Nations, which prohibits the use of force and manages relations between states on the basis of peaceful international cooperation. In joining this organization the Arab and Islamic states abandoned, *de jure*, the distinction between the world of Islam and the world of war. They had, in fact, abandoned the distinction a long time ago: from the late Middle Ages onwards the Islamic countries ceased trying to propagate Islam by violent means. Since the end of the 19th century they have been victims of colonial violence directed against them rather than active proponents of worldwide Islamization.

Moreover, Western countries can no longer be considered a "house of war". There are many Muslims who live in these countries in conditions very different from those of the Middle Ages. They are free to worship there as they see fit; in fact they are sometimes freer from persecution than in Muslim states. One of the best known intellectuals now living in Europe, Tariq Ramadan, has proposed that the Muslims living in these countries consider the West as a "house of witnessing", where they can practice their Islamic faith pacifically. Only Islamic radicalism continues to conceive the world in terms of the traditional distinctions, making the West a house of war.

We can now turn to the problem of political violence in relation to the events of September 11. Does there exist, in Islam, a theory of political murder? If so, is the systematic elimination of political adversaries justified? Is there, in Islam, a potentially dangerous political "essence" – analogous to the essence of which Carl Schmitt speaks – that distinguishes between friend and foe, that defines communities in existential terms, thereby legitimizing *status religionis* rather than *status naturalis*, the right to give or receive death?[1]

Within Islam we can identify three different rationalities of violence. The first two are linked to holy war, the third to war waged in the general interest. But all three entail a cognitive process that evokes an enemy. This process produces three logical alternatives: Islam or death; Islam or submission; repentance or death.

Missionary rationality: Islam or death

As regards pagans, infidels and polytheists, the alternative is clear-cut: Islam or death. We will name this "missionary rationality", an element that Weber left completely aside in concentrating on the financial gains to be won by territorial expansion. The duty to kill polytheists is a well established tradition. It is founded on several verses, in particular a verse that grants immunity in such cases, known as the verse "of the sword". The pagans' lives are be saved only if they accept Islam: "Oh Prophet! strive hard against the Unbelievers and the Hypocrites; be firm against them!" (9: 73).[2] To be sure, these instructions are offset by 124 other verses that call on Muslims to be patient and tolerant, prompt to grant amnesty and pardon. Nonetheless, the verse in question is of capital importance as it figures in the ninth *surah* of the Koran which promises the prophet immunity (*barâa*) after the latter had agreed to a truce with the infidels of Mecca: "But when the forbidden months are past, then fight and slay the Pagans wherever ye find them, and seize them, beleaguer them, and lie in wait for them..." (9:5). Classical exegesis has canonized this interpretation, considering that this single verse serves to repeal the verses (between 114 and 124 of them) that preach tolerance and liberality in dealings with unbelievers. It precisely these latter verses that those who advocate a charitable interpretation of the Koran (those who can be termed "Spinozists") have emphasized.

Let us take a closer look at the historical context in which the "Islam or death" alternative was first formulated. During the battle of Bedr (624 AD), the prophet, who emerged victorious, took fifty prisoners among whom were members of his own family and nobles of the Koraysh tribe, his own tribe. Yet they were unbelievers. The prophet consulted his companions. Omar was in favour of killing them, Abu Bakr of sparing them. The prophet hesitated. After comparing Omar to Noah and Moses who implored their Lord to annihilate their enemies – and Abu Bakr to Abraham and Jesus who pleaded with their Lord for indulgence and mercy – he decided to ransom the Koraysh nobles for the benefit of the poor and destitute population recently converted. God then intervened, addressing his messenger in reproachful terms: What! You fight to acquire booty and not in order to have the religion of Allah reign supreme above all others? And the text continues: "It is not fitting for a Prophet that he should have prisoners of war until he hath thoroughly subdued the land." And further: "Had it not been for a previous ordainment from Allah, a severe penalty would have reached you for the (ransom) that ye took" (8: 67-68). Since that time, tradition has determined the alternatives that polytheists face: Islam or death. Yet later on, certain theorists, doubtless aware of the brutal nature of the dilemma, amended it by adding on other alternatives to which the conquerors could have recourse, alternatives that were based on a different verse of the Koran: the victors could choose between putting captive unbelievers to death, ransoming them, making slaves of them, or pardoning them (47:4).

Surah Nine of the Koran has become the centrepiece of the Islamist world view. It was Sayyid Qutb who provided the theoretical basis, likening the Muslims living in the land of Islam to infidels living in the age of paganism and polytheism. The theory, known as the "new *jahiliyya* (pre-Islamic paganism)", can serve to justify the murder of those branded as tyrants such as, for example, Anwar Sadat.

The rationality that applies to the People of the Book: Islam or submission

The second alternative is invoked in regard to the People of the Book: Jews and Christians to whom should be added the Sabeans, descendants of the people of the Saba kingdom, the Samaritans, and the Persian Zoroastrians, who are said to have a "semblance" of a Book, a "quasi-Book" so to speak. Their status is established by the Koran: "Fight those who believe not in Allah nor the Last Day, nor hold that forbidden which hath been forbidden by Allah and his Messenger, nor acknowledge the Religion of Truth, from among the People of the Book, until they pay the *Jizyah* with willing submission and feel themselves subdued" (9:29). The text is clear, and the successive interpretations have constantly reaffirmed the duty to combat the People of the Book. The only positive note is struck when interpreters of the text point out that "subdued" signifies, by way of a euphemism, that they have come under Islamic rule.

The alternative presented is without doubt an unfortunate one, but it is nonetheless not an exclusive one - that is, it is not a declaration of war aiming to exterminate them. It should rather be characterized as form of residual tolerance, often codified by protective treaties between Muslims and the People of the Book.

Nonetheless the point of departure was a state of war between Muslims and Jews. To be more specific, in Yadhreb, later to become Medina, two Arab tribes recently converted to Islam lived side by side, but torn by ancestral tribal competition: the Awz and the Khazrej. Next door lived three Jewish tribes: the Bani Qaynoqâ, the Bani Nadhîr and the Bani Qorayzha. The first two Jewish tribes were driven out in 624 and 625, and the third was literally decimated two years later. The classical historian of Islam Tabari has recounted how these wars were waged: how people died, abdicated, were converted or fled. Yet he points out that the rising onset of violence never reached the level of collective extermination. So why was such wrongdoing committed?

In fact, the Jews were blamed for having reached an understanding with the Arab polytheists of Mecca during the Battle of the Trenches (627), known as the Battle of Khandag in reference to the name of the trench that the converts had dug to protect Yadhreb. Once the troops from Mecca had been driven back that very afternoon, the prophet fell upon the Bani Qorayzha. But according to Tabari, this explanation, which is political in nature, does not settle the question, because the prophet was visited by the Angel Gabriel who urged him to advance on the Jews and informed him that the Angels had decided it was not the time to lay down arms.[3] The Koran conserves traces of this victory: "And those People of the Book who aided them — Allah did take them down from their strongholds and cast terror into their hearts, (so that) some ye slew, and some ye made prisoners" (33:26).

In these two types of rationality, missionary and territorial subjugation, the combatants abide by *jus in bellum,* the law of just war which includes the ultimatum, the siege, and the use of the tactical methods necessary to ensure victory. As for treachery, perfidy, the use of poisoned arrows, the destruction of homes, and other unacceptable methods, they are subjects of discussion among legal scholars. Some are prepared to admit them; others are not. In the course of hostilities, the enemy must, whatever the circumstances, be treated with justice (5: 2), respect (6: 109) and mercy (2: 195). In case of victory, non-combatants, women, children, the aged, monks, servants and slaves are to be held as prisoners. They are considered, along with their belongings, as part of the war booty. They can be pardoned, reduced to slavery, or sold, or can pay a ransom to be liberated. If they are monotheists they are required to pay the head tax.

It should be remembered that the people of the (revealed) Book had a double status: a theological status that was looked upon with suspicion and a legal status that afforded them protection. Theologically speaking they were, at one and the same time, friends and enemies. Friends because their Books, their beliefs and their tales were considered as sources of authority, inspiration and undeniable scriptural proof for Muslims. Yet enemies because it was thought they had distorted the sense of the Scriptures and were thus classified alongside the hypocrites, the liars and the unjust. Legally their treatment varied according to whether they were armed or not. If they were armed they were treated according to the laws of war: death to combatants and distribution of their goods as war booty. If they were unarmed, they were afforded "protection": they were included in the "house" of Islam, but not in the "community" of Muslims. They were required to pay the head tax, called *jeziya*, a tax levied on all males considered sane of mind, but not on women, children, the demented, slaves and those suspected of being hermaphrodites, considered as accessory persons lacking the autonomous judicial status of individuals. In exchange, they could worship as they pleased – as an inferior and demeaned people.

Protection, autonomy, and payment of the head tax: such were the three principles that determined the rules by which they were to be governed. It is this system that made it possible for Medieval Islam to administer the ethnic and religious minorities in a great number of regions – minorities that have in many regions conserved their status up to the present time, to the extent that Islam has been referred to as a mosaic of ethnic minorities and religious communities. It is only since modern times, when Islamic nations, pressured by Europe, adopted charters such as the Turkish Khatt Homayun in 1839 and the Tunisian pact of 1957, that the People of the Book were accorded full citizenship rights akin to those enjoyed by Muslims.[4]

The fires of holy war, "this most typical of Muslim popular epics" – to quote Massignon[5] – were rekindled in the second stage of nationalism in rebellion against the colonizer considered as a reincarnation of the crusader. Once independence was won, the new regimes attempted to redirect the *jihad* as a struggle against poverty and backwardness. Liberal theologians, for their part, reminded the faithful that the meaning of the *jihad* was first and foremost a struggle to be waged against oneself in order to attain a great degree of perfection. However, their reminders did not succeed in dampening the people's ardour, nor in banishing from popular religious mythology the myth of the combatant who offers himself up as a martyr to the cause, eager to enter the promised Paradise which would be open to him regardless of whether or not he had, in the course of his life on earth, proved faithful to Islamic precepts.

War would be adopted in the third instance by radical Islamism. A new era of "the rebellion of the faithful" is inaugurated. By way of example, the emir of the Egyptian terrorist group, "Anathema and Apostasy", replied in 1977 with disconcerting frankness to a question asked of him by a judge of the National Security Court: "As far as the war against the Jews is concerned, it is, from a legal point of view, a duty that belongs the Islamic community as a whole, and we will put it into effect, God willing, once we are in power".[6] Thus was forged once again a chain of war, extending from the Hamas movement to the Algerian GIA, including "death-dealing Shiism" fascinated by the sacrifice of Imam Hussein.[7] There was talk at this time of a type of violence motivated by a redeeming sense of despair, as a reaction against a society tempted more by the lures of pleasure than by religious rigour! No doubt there is some truth in this. In any case, the over-whelming proof is there to be seen: foreigners, tourists, followers of other religions, and NGO workers were classified without distinction as People of the Book – as crusaders, blasphemers, colonial henchmen etc.[8] And the avowed intent was simple: the conversion of humanity to "ummanity" (the community of Muslims on earth).[9]

To be sure, one can legitimately object to the grouping into one category of, for instance, tourists, the People of the Book, and the crusaders. The status of *dhimmis* (those protected) no longer exists in contemporary Islam, and foreigners are subject to the rule of modern law. In fact, classical Islam raised the figure of the foreigner to the level of the sublime; he was treated with the legendary hospitality of the Arabs, an ethic of Bedouin honour known as *al-muruwa*, reserved for travellers and beggars. Protection, honour, exchange of favours, sacrifice, loyalty and hospitality were the principles that governed the *muruwa*. Goldhizer, who served as a source for Weber, went so far as to consider the *muruwa* a chivalric ethic, the *virtus latine*.[10] The heights of the sublime are attained in certain literary works, in particular in a text by Tawhîdi, a tenth-century author, dealing with foreignness to oneself: "The stranger is he who is a stranger in his very strangeness!"

Nonetheless, once the question is set in a judicial context, the mythical figure of the foreigner-as-guest disappears, to be replaced by that of the protected person or the crusader enemy. But if a person who enjoys protection breaks the contract that binds him by refusing, even without violence, to pay the tribute that is owed, he is, in the best of cases, pardoned by the imam or driven out of Islamic territory, *manu militari* if necessary – and in the worst of cases, put to death or reduced to slavery. Protection can be accorded to an enemy warrior (*harbî*), provided that the Muslim grants him an *amân*, a safe-conduct that ensures that his life and belongings will be protected in accord-ance with the principle of respect for the pledged word.[11] He can reside up to one year on Islamic soil, without having to pay tribute, but without benefiting from the protection that is afforded the People of the Book. If any such person takes up arms, he is once again considered as an enemy.

Weber could not understand, as it was described, the transformation of the rationality of territorial expansion for financial gain into a missionary rationality. Radical Islamism is far more obsessed by religious sedition that by the opportunity to reap economic benefits. Today the rhetoric of Islamist violence condones the execution of the innocent as if the crusades were still "a chapter of contemporary history".[12] In classical times, the situation was clearer: the Franks, as they were crusaders, paid with their lives[13] or else were forced to pay for a safe-conduct,[14] a form of ransom that was collected by the league of Assassins whose members – paradoxically – were disguised as monks. It was so anchored in custom that it sometimes happened, according to Lewis, that the Assassins themselves paid the tribute to the Franks!

Today the question is to determine who must pay a protection tax or a safe-conduct tax and to whom. And if a non-Muslim should venture to proclaim that he is an atheist, he will no longer be classed among the People of the Book, but considered as a pagan for whom death is the lawful end.

State rationality: repentance or death

The third way of legitimizing violence belongs to an aspect of Weber's theory of state rationality, namely the monopoly of the use of force that rightly belongs to the nation. In this context, it is Muslims versus Muslims, the orthodox versus the heretics, or, to use a more modern expression, the dominant versus the dominated. The choice here is between repentance or death. The issues at stake are similar to those that are of concern in Islam today: law and order and the genuine precepts of Islam. The accounts of the schisms that have torn Islam apart are complex – and often of little immediate interest. Limiting our analysis to cases that have a direct bearing on the contemporary situation, we will mention but three: violation of the law, revolt and apostasy. Except that – and the point to be made is crucial for our understanding – these acts of violence are not part of a holy war, but come under the heading of wars in the general interest, the purpose of which is the restoration of religious law and order.

But first of all, on what divine commandment do Muslims base their right to make war? The Koran here provides the appropriate answer: "If two parties among the Believers fall into a quarrel, make ye peace between them: but if one of them transgresses beyond bounds against the other, then fight ye (all) against the one that transgresses until it complies with the command of Allah" (49: 9). The Koran uses the verb *baghat*, the true sense of which is to transgress, break the peace, overstep the limits, whereas some translations uses a far narrower term: to rebel. *Baghat* is the original term used in classical Islam to describe what the authorities today refer to as armed heretical gangs: they are those who are addicted to transgression or disobedience (*ahl al-bagha*), those who disobey state authority, not as individuals but as members of gangs. Some people go as far as to assert that the *jihad* waged against the extremists is "as valid, if not more valid than the *jihad* waged against infidels."[15] According to public law they constitute the enemy, except that, since they are Muslims, the war against them is one of general interest. Since it is thus a war between allies, once defeated, they are accepted by the authorities. Their goods are given back to them, their dead are anointed and they are buried in Islamic cemeteries accompanied by the traditional rites. To be sure, the principles of *jus in bellum* that apply to conflicts between brothers are not always in practice respected. Nonetheless, the fact that these principles have been codified can be considered as a guarantee, even if not all public authorities are in a position to put them into effect.

The second justification employed by the state to re-establish law and order is the fight against underworld and gangster revolts. In classical times they were known as the *muhâribun*, brigands and troublemakers who endangered freedom of movement. The legal basis of the struggle against them is to be found in a verse of the Koran which specifies the four punishments to which these enemies of public order could be liable: death, crucifixion, amputation of the right hand and the left foot, or exile (5:33). In fact the treatment they are accorded falls somewhere between these four sanctions and repentance. Today, many Arab states have signed the Convention against Torture and Cruel, Inhuman or Degrading Treatment or Punishment.[16] However, the acceptance of this convention is only a formality that entails no practical consequences, all the more so because the Sharia remains the basic norm for many Arab states.

Then there is a third category: apostasy. The apostate is said to be a *murtad*, or renegade. The Koran has nothing to say as to his status, but the prophet is said to have once declared: "He who abandons his religion, kill him!" That the prophet actually said these words is disputed and debated, for it is highly likely that the dictum was concocted after the fact to justify the killing of the first apostates. The latter were Arab tribes converted to Islam who, once the prophet died, renounced their new faith. The first caliph, Abu Bakr (632-634), waged a merciless war against them ("the apostate wars"). The precedent was accepted as authoritative, but the category of apostasy was to be inordinately enlarged.

Kerou has analyzed the process of exclusion. Starting with the *fatwas* (consultations) for blasphemy and apostasy launched against Salman Rushdie, the academic Hamed Abu Zeyd and Nobel Prize winner Naguib Mahfouz, he reveals by what mechanisms blasphemy against God, insult in regard to the prophet and apostasy are considered as the equivalent of infidelity (*kufr*) and thus become subject to the death penalty.[17] One might be tempted to think that this process was limited to certain specific categories, were it not for the fact that the list of what was considered as loss of faith grew all out of proportion: throwing away a copy of the Koran, dressing like an unbeliever, blaspheming, treating forbidden practices such as drinking alcohol as licit, etc.

Today the "renegades" are unwed women, acculturated laymen, artists who "treat life lightly".[18] It was in this spirit that Sheik Ghazali, the Egyptian Islamist, testified in the name of the defendants before the Supreme Security Court of Egypt that was conducting preliminary inquiries into the murder of the secularist F. Fouda by Islamic Jihad in 1992. He declared that the sentence to be applied to an apostate was death, unless the latter repented, and furthermore claimed that the killer of an apostate should go unpunished since in killing a renegade he was only acting to replace the political authorities who were lax in fulfilling their duties.[19] The Islamic regimes are in agreement when it comes to such matters, since the "Declaration of the Rights of Man in Islam", drawn up in 1992 under the auspices of the OIC (the Organization of the Islamic Conference that brings together the Islamic states) asserts in Article 10 the very same principle: it is forbidden to change religions because Islam is the "natural" religion (dîn al-fitra). One can understand once again how the state enters into competition with the radicals in order to keep for itself jurisdiction concerning the granting of pardons and the ethics of salvation.

Let us imagine for a moment what apostasy involves: the apostate cannot escape death by paying a compensatory fine; the animals that the apostate slaughters are not fit to be eaten; marriage is forbidden him – whereas in the case of those who enjoy a protected status there are no such prohibitions. In civil terms, the apostate does not exist: his marriage is annulled, he loses the right to serve as guardian or tutor, he cannot inherit. Even the rules pertaining to a just war are denied him: he can be attacked from in front or from behind; no truce will be granted him; it is legal to shed his blood in combat or when he is taken prisoner; his belongings are treated as booty; he does not even deserve the status of a slave.

Finally, even though battle here is conducted in the general interest, the fate reserved for the apostate is harsher than the treatment reserved for the polytheist. The circle of violence returns once again to death. Did the states that have adhered to the Declaration of the

Rights of Man in Islam take this into account? Probably not; but the radicals certainly did! Does such an approach go as far as to include terrorism, the fourth stage of its evolution? The reply has not yet been decided. For terrorism can find its place in the context of the three teleological rationalities, while at the same time deriving justification as a legitimate form of violence.

Is there a theory of terrorism in Islam?

It is generally accepted that Islam is not Islamism and that Islamism is not terrorism. In addition, terrorism is a catchall concept that has been stretched to the point where it results in an amalgam between the most varied kinds of violence, both targeted and random (hostage taking, attacks on soldiers, suicide attacks, and other criminal acts...).[20] It is also true that systematic recourse to murder – to intentional but depersonalized homicide – is a phenomenon that has emerged in the context of recent history: revolutionary terror, nationalism and democracy.[21] In "pre-modern" times there already existed a tradition of homicide linked to political causes, for the most part tyrannicide, the first example of which dates from roughly 1200 BC, during the reign of the Judges: the Benjamite Ehud liberating Israel from the bonds of Eglôn, king of Moab, or again the campaign of assassinations practiced by the Zealots and the Assassins of Islam (from which we have derived the modern term "assassin"), not to mention the institutionalized violence of the Catholic Church.[22]

Classical Islam did not have specific terms for what the modern states define as extremism (tatarruf), terrorism (irhâb), or assassination (ightiyâl). Classical Islam preferred the term ghuluw (exaggeration, excess). It applied to all those attitudes that were opposed to a certain moderate Islam that abhorred the excessive (2: 143), whether it concerned religious ardour or heretical opinions. The reasoning is simple: the prophet was sent to make life easier and less burdensome for the believer.[23] It is the very essence of mesotos (wasat) and of Oikonomia (iqtisâd) that was a source of glory for the prophet, the "mirror of Princes" in Islam. In politics the word *ghuluw* became the term used to refer to the excesses of Shiism (*ghulât-shîa*). Unlike the ordinary Shiites who considered the imam a descendant of the prophet (on the basis of the Koran and Mohamed's last will), one sect went well beyond, adding on three additional principles: incarnation or infusion (the imam incarnates the divine spirit); metempsychosis (the transmission of prophecy); and libertinism (the refusal to practice the religious rites). Such were the beliefs of the Assassins (*hashâshin*) who had proclaimed on 8 August 1164 the end of the Sharia and the coming of the "great resurrection (*al-qiyâma al-kobra*)".[24] We could say – with all due respect for contextual differences – that they took refuge in the inaccessible mountain heights of Alamut, in a manner roughly similar to that of Bin Laden in Afghanistan.

It was only a step from that stage to the decreeing of assassination, a step that political Islam took early on. Not that easily, it must be said, for if the Koran accepts violence in many of its forms, it disapproves of assassination, the premeditated treacherous attack, for "God has no love for the unbelieving traitor" (32: 38). This verse has been taken by classical scholars – basing their interpretation on the particular circumstances in which it occurs – to mean that assassination (*fatk* or *ightiyâl*) is forbidden: the believers had consulted Mohammed to know if they were authorized to kill infidels by treachery; and the prophet had forbidden it. Nonetheless, no less than seven murders had taken place, killings conducted by surprise and trickery of five Jews (one of whom was a woman) and two inhabitants of Mecca who had blasphemed against Mohammed at Medina. Was the order to kill them given by Mohammed? Ashmawy, writing as a Muslim secularist, denies it.[25] Classical interpretations downplayed the assassination, considering it as dictated by the ultimate end to be achieved, as a war stratagem employed by the prophet before the definitive victory of Islam. According to Tabari the tactic employed remains practically always the same: cultivate one or two people close to the victim to win his confidence, draw him into a trap preferably at night, and then execute him so as to strike terror into the enemy's heart. But suicide attacks (not to be confused with death in combat) are forbidden. Moreover, the ban on suicide stems from the same principle of respect for life (4: 29-30) and the responsibility for a man to be conscious of the acts that he performs (74: 38) and responsible even for the organs of his body: "...for every act of hearing, or of seeing, or of the heart will be enquired into (on the Day of Reckoning)" (17: 36). Once Islam had definitively triumphed, terrorism was eliminated from the classical theory of war.[26]

In fact, only the outlawed unorthodox sects were to have recourse to terrorism. In the case of Kharijism, a sect that rejected the caliphate of Ali as invalid, terrorism was adopted as a revolutionary strategy according to a sequential pattern that ascended through four phases, determined in each case by the degree of repression to which they were subjected: the devout stage (the sect is reduced to silence); the secret stage (the sect has difficulty surviving); the resistance stage (armed struggle); and finally the stage of glory when the minority, considering itself as the true house of Islam, triumphs over the house of war. On the contrary, the Shiites, pursued by relentless repression, withdrew behind a theory of dissimulation (taqiyya), which consisted of hiding their allegiance to Ali, until the day when Khomeini put an end to it in the 1960s.

Today, political assassinations have resumed in the second (national) phase. The methods employed in the East may be no more bloody or cruel than those of other peoples; but the list of assassinations is fairly extensive.[27] Sunni radicalism, along with Islamic Jihad, Hamas, the Taliban and the GIA, has taken over the implementation of the third and fourth stages. However, terrorism, for its adepts, remains a means towards an end, though its "ethical" status is open to question, even in terms of an Islamic moral code that admits strategic deviations. This is proved by the difficulties that the Shiite clergy encounter when attempting to provide a religious basis for hostage taking or justification for the terror that struck the Twin Towers. Their leaders prefer to take refuge in *ad hoc* justifications such as the use of hostages as means of obtaining prisoner exchange.[28] Nonetheless, despite the subterfuges that allow them to avoid being considered as the sponsors of assassinations, it must be said that recourse to exceptional methods forms part of the same canon: the designation of the enemy (the proud) and those who are friends (the deprived), as well as the means (terror) and the final objective (an Islamic republic).

Today's Islamic terrorism no doubt has modern sociological roots, against which the Islamic governments, when they are taken as targets – and, as is often the case, considered as the reason for attacks – are powerless, despite their constant condemnations.[29] Nonetheless, between yesterday's Assassins and today's commandos there exists a community of purpose, inspired as they both are by "the same impatient, zealous will to rid the community of all foreign influence",[30] even if – and the point cannot be overemphasized – there are profound differences between these two forms of extremism. Accepting the risk that a mere "elective affinity" may be transformed into a hastily concluded parallel, the Islamists make much of the precedents established in the past in order to justify the physical elimination of their adversaries. Taking refuge in their distance from the impious world, they model their behaviour strictly on the rules of the holy war, launching their attacks against material goods and the lives of innocents. From tyrannicide to terrorism, via the holy war, they repeat all the phases of the history of violence, almost indifferent to the passage of time. It matters little if terrorism, in the final analysis, is incapable of overthrowing the regimes in power, as history has shown us. The strategy deteriorates into scattered blows that are not really essential for the armed gangs to survive.

How do ideas resist the test of history? Neither Nietzsche's genealogy nor Foucault's archaeology provides an answer to that question. From the very beginnings of Islam the first questionings of religiosity appeared and were to endure: in what mode should one live one's salvation and deliverance? By simply professing belief in God and in

Mohammed or, in addition, by performing duties that are indispensable and giving oneself over to resolute meditation? What is the difference between universal faith (*imân*) and Islam, which is a specific religion? The theories concerning a liberal Islam have unfortunately not put an end to the exaggerations that have shaken Islam. From the murder of the first caliphs (Othman and Ali) to the recent attacks, it is always the same foundational gesture, serving at one and the same time as a mobilizing myth, an eschatological expectation and a utopia to be achieved.

None of the explanations of violence can do away with our intuition: a society does have the capacity to neutralize "the violence that stems from conviction", instead of allowing the destructive impulse to prey on it. Wellhausen, who served as mentor to Weber, began his history of the Arab Empire by asserting that religion was the specific feature of these societies.[31] According to Pier-Cesare Bori's interpretation of religious texts, the Text matures with its readers as a mother comes to full maturity as her children grow.[32] However it would seem as if Islam, having made the religious element "the raison d'être of the state, the principle of unity, and the theory of the nation",[33] regressed in its reading. Or, to put it in more optimistic terms, the Text and its readers have not grown up together harmoniously. Will secularized democracy be capable of reconciling Islam and the world? At any rate, it is clear today that Islam will be increasingly incapable of maturing if it adheres to radical fundamentalism, after having failed in its attempt to find its true measure without recourse to fundamentalism and even in opposition to it.

Conclusion

The tension between the political and the hieratic remains a crucial question for Islam today. It is this tension that has created a situation in which fundamentalists and dictatorial regimes are now more than ever locked in competition for the monopoly of divine grace. The legalism of the Sharia, instead of being a theocratic form of law that provides a

stable base for commercial relations, has become for the fundamentalists a passion fed by emotional and nostalgic rationalization. It is this
spirit that has driven the fundamentalists to rebel against Islamic regimes and to consider that the lands of Islam in which the Sharia is not
strictly applied are lands in the hands of infidels. As for *fatwas*, they
have become a means of creating mandatory judicial commands – ar-
bitrary, casuistical and subjective – and no longer the justice dispensed
by a Qadi. With regard to non-Muslims, the objective of holy war is
no longer the payment of tribute or the conquest of feudal domains,
but instead has become, like the crusades, an undertaking pursued according to the Augustinian maxim *cogite entrare*. The fundamentalist
combatant for the true faith is no longer a warrior attached to the simple pleasures of life here on earth, but a messianic, death-dealing hero
who sacrifices his life on the altar of God, spurred on by the promise
of the eternal salvation of his soul in paradise. Is it a true salvation, a
redemption, a predestination, or is it a negative transfiguration of the
rationale of deliverance? The question remains open.

2

THE IMPOSSIBLE PALESTINIAN MARTYR STRATEGY: VICTIMIZATION AND SUICIDE ATTACKS

Laetitia Bucaille

The random suicide attacks launched against Israeli civilians have provoked indignation and incomprehension in the Western world. Considered as a basically illegitimate means of political combat, such terror attacks have been condemned by political and religious figures[1] as well as by a certain number of Palestinian intellectuals.[2] Above and beyond moral condemnation, public opinion is astonished by the spectacle of young people who choose to turn themselves into human bombs, which is seen as irrational. Some observers have concluded that the suicide bombers are the prey of cynical, manipulative political leaders, skilled in producing killing machines. Others consider that the suicide attacks are the ultimate expression of the Palestinians' distress, mired in poverty with no hope for the future. These approaches to the problem are simplifications that do not take into account the political, social and psychological factors that underlie such acts or explain the widespread character of this phenomenon that continues unabated and enlists a growing number of followers. Analyzing the suicide attacks in no way implies justifying them: the purpose here is to lay bare the underlying logic that precipitates radical violence.

We will concentrate on the suicide bomber phenomenon during the 1990s in the context of the Al-Aqsa Intifada. The first suicide attacks were launched in April 1994 by the Islamic Resistance Movement (Hamas), which had never accepted the Oslo Peace Accords. By this unprecedented strategy, Hamas intended to avenge the Palestinians killed in the Hebron massacre.[3] Between April 1994 and October 1998, Islamic Jihad and Hamas carried out sixteen attacks of this kind,[4] justified as responses to Israeli aggression, attacks that weighed heavily on the negotiations then underway between the Palestinian Authority and the Israeli government. During the Al-Aqsa Intifada the Islamist movements stepped up the rhythm. In the year 2001 alone, Hamas and the Islamic Jihad carried out eighty such operations.[5] Starting in 2001 members of Fatah, which supported the peace process and which had condemned attacks on Israeli civilians, began launching suicide attacks of their own within Israeli borders.

It has already been shown that the rationale underlying the suicide attacks is both religious and political in origin.[6] The organizers of these operations and those that carry them out justify their acts in both spiritual and nationalist terms, as if neither of these frameworks was sufficient in and of itself to legitimate their tactics. The initiative for the attacks and for their increasing number stems from decisions taken by politico-military groups; but their advent is the result as well of an evolution of the Palestinians' system of beliefs, their representations and their view of the world.

Our hypothesis is that the intensification of suicide attacks constitutes an attempt on the part of the Palestinians to alter their relationship with the world at large and redefine their place in history. Forced to conclude that they had been unable to convince international public opinion and the governing powers of the planet that they were indeed victims, they attempted to transform their very weakness into a political weapon, without however entirely abandoning their aim of acquiring victim status. By choosing a policy of murderous violence against Israeli civilians, the paramilitary organizations revealed the incapacity of their society and of their leaders to create and develop a winning strategy of national liberation.

The uncertain strategies of the Palestinian national struggle

The first Intifada (1978–93) mobilized Palestinian society as a whole in support of an innovative form of struggle founded basically on civil disobedience with little recourse to violence. On the other hand, the revolt that started in the Palestinian Territories in September 2000 failed to develop a coherent organization, hesitating between very different types of initiatives which, taken together, resulted in an inconsistent strategy.

The figure of the "martyr" as the rallying point of national unity. The vagueness of the concept of "martyr" in Palestinian society has had the unexpected effect of placing all the dead in the same category. Thus a shahid can be a civilian non-combatant felled by Israeli soldiers' bullets as well as a suicide bomber who deliberately kills himself as a way of killing others. The youngster who throws stones and the combatant who fires his M16 at a military checkpoint and dies under the barrage of return fire are also known as "martyrs". Does the confusion reveal an unwillingness to make distinctions? When all the dead are honoured, whatever the circumstances, no single type of death in the struggle against Israel is given a unique form of legitimacy. In the current language of the Palestinians, the "martyr" is both an innocent victim and a hero who risks his life or dies in combat.

The honours accorded Palestinians killed "by mistake" when they were not engaged in combat or resistance indicate the intent to invest them with political and national significance. The essential characteristics of the concept of "martyr" – the deliberate choice to accept suffering and death in the pursuit of a struggle for a political or religious cause – is here left out. The attacks launched by Israeli soldiers or settlers against unarmed Palestinian civilians suffice for the death of the latter to be considered as a sacrifice for the community as a whole. It is thus the initiative taken by the Israeli enemy and not the behaviour or the status of the Palestinian that defines the category of "martyr". This outlook is rooted in the Palestinians' political *imaginaire* that determines the image of their community and its relation to the world.

First of all, the fact that an unarmed civilian is struck down by the fire of a powerful enemy proves, in the eyes of the Palestinians, that they risk their lives by the very fact that they are members of their political community. The identity of the Palestinian nation is thus based on the recognition that they are all potential victims and that, for all of them, the threat can become a reality at any moment. In this way the Palestinians can keep the myth of national unity alive.

In addition, the fact of considering non-active civilians as "martyrs" lends credence to the interpretation of the struggle as one between inoffensive Palestinians and all-powerful Israelis, and so reinforces the idea of an overwhelming disproportion in strength between the oppressors and the oppressed.

The aura attached to the figure of the "martyr" is more than evident in the attitudes that have developed among the young between the ages of 15 and 24, those whom we could call "the younger brothers". This generation had witnessed the first Intifada as children. They were deeply impressed by the violence of the counterattacks of the Israeli army, and the memories of the "heroes" killed for the cause were still vivid. When asked to express their personal ambitions and their future plans many of these adolescents asserted that they wanted to become "martyrs", without giving any precise meaning to the term.[7]

In a war situation it is not unusual for young people to declare their patriotism and to sign up for combat at the risk of their lives. Yet the terse character of these young people's reply is surprising. In evoking the figure of the "martyr", the "younger brothers" were simply expressing their desire to sacrifice their lives. They provided no details as to how their deaths would come about, nor as to what impact it might have on their adversaries. They embraced the ascetic ideal of sacrifice for the community, but left aside the question of the fight against the enemy. Questions as to the effectiveness of the attack being planned, or the scale of the damage to be inflicted on the enemy, were not brought up. The adolescents who replied in these terms gave the impression that their chief objective was to achieve a place of honour and prestige in their political community rather than to win a battle in the war against Israeli.

During the first months of the Al-Asqa Intifada, the "younger brothers" were in the forefront of the national struggle. Taking as model the uprising sparked by their elders in the late 1980s, they repeated the gesture that had become famous throughout the world, throwing stones: a gesture, however, that in its initial context had not been the essential aspect of the mobilization but only its outward form. Taken out of the framework of a basic strategy of civil disobedience, the tactic adopted by the stone throwers did not have the same significance. In addition it verged on the absurd, since the Israeli Army mobilized its forces as never before in order to suppress all forms of revolt in the Territories. On an operational level, the tactic of throwing stones at checkpoints or Israeli military outposts was a failure; the stones hardly ever reached their intended targets, which were too far away or equipped with sophisticated protective gear. Besides being ineffective, these tactics proved to be counter-productive since dozens of the young people armed with these projectiles were killed by Israeli Army fire.[8] In terms of combat tactics, the ratio of cost to result was largely in the adversary's favour.

The effectiveness of this type of operation thus lay solely in its symbolic significance, since the strategy of stone throwing was to become inseparable from the figure of the "martyr". The choice of this form of combat should not, however, be attributed simply to the lack of means at these youngsters' disposal. It draws first of all on a political culture. Stone-throwing is not only seen as a form of tribute paid to the heroes of the past struggle – a glorious but unfinished struggle – of the first Intifada against the occupation; in addition, this image has been overlaid with that of the martyrdom of Hamas and Islamic Jihad suicide attacks. These movements began their suicide attacks against Israeli civilians at the very moment when, in 1994, Palestinian autonomy became a reality. The strategy of the Islamist movements was controversial within Palestinian society: first of all it did not yield any significant gains in the struggle against Israel, and in addition it damaged the image of the Palestinians in the eyes of the international community whose support they sought. Finally, and above all, by challenging the monopoly control of violence that the Palestinian Authority sought to impose, the Islamist operations aggravated tensions in the domestic policy arena. Between 1994 and 2000, a serious conflict of legitimacy sprung up between the supporters of negotiations with Israel and the opponents of the Oslo Accords, a conflict that on occasion came close to getting out of hand.

The "gratuitous" immolation of the young stone throwers opened the way for a reestablishment of unanimity embodied in the emergence of a new figure of the "martyr". Confronted by the death of members of the Palestinian community, consensus and cohesion were bound to be reinforced. By assuming the role of victim, however, the Palestinians risked losing their capacity to develop a collective project for national liberation. It is not the first time in their history that Palestinians have accepted – and even proclaimed – defeat. It is a common sight for Palestinians, especially children and adolescents, to mimic the V for Victory sign for the benefit of the photographers and cameramen of the foreign press, even in cases of defeat at the hands of the Israelis: for example, when they flash the V in front of the ruins of their homes destroyed by the Israeli Army. As early as 1983, the PLO forces, filmed for television as they were leaving Beirut, had given the two-finger salute, even though they had been routed and forced to withdraw. More recently, Yasser Arafat, under the threat of expulsion and perhaps even physical elimination by the Israelis, repeated the symbol. From their earliest age Palestinians have constantly repeated the gesture, summoning the foreigner to witness the loser's honour by brandishing the sign of a moral victory.[9]

Convincing the world that the Palestinians are victims. During the first months of the Intifada, the scenes that one saw on television demonstrated the very unequal balance between opposing forces, conveying the idea that the conflict could be reduced to a confrontation between the courage of Palestinian civilians and the ferocity of Israeli soldiers. In this sense the Palestinians, rather than relying on the astuteness of the guerrillas who were defying Israeli military forces, counted on a political victory that would be evident in the eyes of international public opinion

One icon, symbolizing the "martyrdom" of the Palestinian people, took on immense importance in the early stages of the Al-Aqsa Intifada. The scene of little Mohamed al-Dura, filmed as he huddled terror stricken against his father, trying to avoid Israeli fire, was the drama of the death of an exemplary victim, the death of an innocent, harmless child. His father, incapable of protecting him, was a figure of almost equal fragility. These images, reproduced worldwide, told the story once again, but in a more striking form: the cruelty of the Israelis, the weakness of the Palestinians whose blood was shed to no purpose. This episode shocked international public opinion and became a fixation for the Palestinians. The local television stations ran the scene over and over again and every family in the West Bank and Gaza could identify with the tragedy and with the role of the perfect victim. The episode, in spite of the pain it occasioned, was a way to force the world to witness deep-seated injustice. Weakness, here, is not a failing that one attempts to hide behind rhetorical eloquence; it is the proof of oppression.

The unequal balance of forces that is the determining factor in Palestinian-Israeli relations can be a danger for the former when the two of them are locked in single combat. On the other hand, it is perhaps possible to take advantage of a position of inferiority if one succeeds in inducing an attitude of compassion on the part of the international community. The backing of Arab societies was a foregone conclusion, but it brought no advantages. Most Palestinians had given up all hope of aid, political or military, coming from the Arab states. For the most part they consider that the public opinion that counts is American or European; yet they have doubts about ever being able to influence significantly the positions taken by these traditional allies of Israel. The ties that bind them are historical, cultural and political. American and European support for the creation of a Jewish state on territory that was part of the British mandate in Palestine stemmed from the concern to make amends for the horrors perpetrated against the Jews during World War Two. The Europeans considered they had a debt to pay; that is why many of them were particularly vigilant about protection of the Israeli state and its citizens. The Palestinians are also aware of the cultural similarities between Israel and the West: the style and level of life in Tel Aviv are close to American or European standards. Finally, the financial, political and military assistance provided to Israel by the Americans illustrates, in forceful and concrete terms, the special ties between the Jewish state and the West.

The Palestinians have no such alliance to fall back on. In attempting to draw attention to the injustice of their fate, what they are expressing is the need to be recognized. They are trying to exchange the worn-out image of the terrorist for that of a people short-changed by history and by the great powers, abused by the Arab states, and today subject to Israeli occupation and repression. The difficulty inherent in such a construct of victimization is that to accept it is tantamount to considering the Israelis as the guilty party. If the Palestinians become the oppressed in the eyes of the world, they run the risk of appearing as the challengers of the Jews, competing for the status of victim that the latter have been granted.

The Palestinians are not unaware of the scale of the genocide perpetrated in Europe in the 1940s. Aware of the suffering undergone by the Jews, they hesitate between two positions. Some are inclined to deny the Jews legitimacy and minimize the question of the Shoah. For these people the Shoah has been blown out of proportion and exploited by Israel for political motives. Others recognize the figure of the Jew as victim, and then make use of it as a basis for comparison. A poster created during the Al-Aqsa Intifada exemplifies the intent to borrow the suffering of the Jews as a means of intensifying the image of Palestinian suffering: it presents two legendary photos side by side, on one side a photo dating from World War Two of a little Jewish boy forced to hold his arms upraised, on the other the image of Mohamed al-Dura huddled against his father. The caption, in English – "The Holocaust Repeated" – underscores the Palestinians' attempt to have the world recognize the extent of their suffering and thus evoke compassion. The aim is to appeal to both the Israelis and the international community, to show the world that it is the Palestinians who are now the people suffering from oppression. The tactic is awkward in that both the Israelis and the Westerners interpret it as an attempt on the part of the Palestinians to equate their suffering with that of the Jews. Yet the suffering of the Jews was the result of a Nazi plan of total extermination; the Palestinians, even if they can convince the world that they are victims, cannot claim to be targeted by a concerted plan of extermination.[10] It is above all the desire to call attention to their plight that has led them to compare their status as victims to that of the Jews.

"If the life of Arabs is of no importance…": inverted rhetoric. Even if European public opinion increasingly indicates its sympathy for the Palestinians' struggle, no Western power has intervened in the region in order to plead the Palestinians' cause and to alter significantly the unequal balance of power from which the latter suffer. The United States, which acts as the sponsor of the peace process, is seen by the Palestinians as the unfailing ally of the Israelis; as for the European Union, even if it often takes a more balanced position in regard to the two parties, the lack of unity and the absence of any real political commitment among its members limits the effectiveness of its initiatives. On the West Bank and in the Gaza Strip, the population is convinced of the indifference and the passivity of the Westerners and considers them to be partial. The inhabitants of the Territories often emphasize

that the foreign media do not treat information concerning the loss of human life in the region in the same manner. The remark made by a mother living in one of the West Bank communities sums up the prevailing opinion: "If an Israeli dies, you can see it on all the TV sets in the world and people cry. When one of ours is killed, hardly any notice is taken."[11]

The Palestinians have the impression that for Westerners Arab deaths are of no great importance. Convinced of their incapacity to elicit a surge of emotion worldwide, they identify with the Western attitude — or what they consider to be the Western attitude — as a way to turn it around. Thus, while they accuse the Americans and the Europeans of being insensitive and are incensed by their lack of compassion, many Palestinians claim to be indifferent to life on earth. Some of the combat strategies adopted by the *shebab*[12] engaged in the Al-Asqa Intifada suggest that they deliberately ran the risk of being killed; this is true of the stone throwers, but also of certain organized groups. In April 2001, members of a Fatah gang who mounted an armed attack on the Tsahal decided not to put on the bullet-proof vests that were readily available.[13] Their objective was not to adopt a more effective means of combat but to take part in a ritual enactment of their unequal struggle against their enemy. For a Palestinian militant true honour consists of offering up one's life. It can thus be seen that the two attitudes — of the Palestinians and the Westerners — feed on each other; the indifference to the death of Palestinians (and of Arabs in general) that is attributed to Westerners is interiorized as a form of stigma. The Islamist-nationalist rhetoric, in particular that of the Hamas, intervenes at this point to turn the stigma around and transform it into a cause for pride: the Palestinians do not fear death and are prepared to sacrifice their lives. When the Palestinians adopt this stance and act in accordance with it, the reaction of Westerners is to conclude that they care little for their lives. They are stunned when they learn that parents allow children and adolescents to run the risk of death and when young people in their twenties decide to blow themselves up in order to kill as many Israelis as possible. The image that each side has of the other contributes to this misunderstanding, widening the gulf of incomprehension and increasing both parties' sense of frustration.

The Palestinian Islamists take as a basic truth the fact that Palestinians and Israelis have different perceptions of death. The former have proved their readiness to accept sacrifice in that they do not hesitate to take considerable risks when confronting their powerful enemy. The latter fear death, even those who serve in the army, since they take all possible precautions in order to limit their losses. This basic truth is then interpreted by the Islamists as the tangible sign of the moral superiority of their religious and political community over the citizens of Israel. They consider the Israelis to be a society of hedonists and materialists that have abandoned moral and religious values, in much the same way as the Americans and Europeans. At this point the Western versus Muslim division re-emerges and accentuates differences.

Convinced that they had found the Israelis' weak spot – the importance they attached to human life – the partisans of the *jihad* decided to employ the spiritual force that they were certain they possessed. Suicide attacks against Israeli civilians appeared then as the way to put to good effect their courage and sense of abnegation and to inflict the most painful possible losses on the enemy. The organizers of the attacks could then witness the impact of the blows they delivered. Anger and pain would then spread to the other side of the Green Line. The repetition of the attacks was a means as well of creating a sense of fear among Israelis, which was taken as yet another sign of their weakness and even of their cowardice.

By inflicting such spectacular blows on the enemy, the combat strategy of the Islamists transformed the "martyr" as victim into the "martyr" as hero. Even if the Islamist approach to Israeli-Palestinian relations and to the solution of the conflict did not become the dominant political line, it affected people's way of seeing things at a moment when the peace process was bogged down. The failure of negotiations led to the conclusion that the Israelis could not be a partner; they were considered once again as the occupying power that had to be got rid of. Israeli military might was well known; Islamist rhetoric provided the a way of facing up to it despite inferiority in material terms. The tendency to describe the Israeli soldiers as frightened and disloyal individuals, radically different from the Palestinian *shebab* with their courage and sense of detachment, had gradually been gaining ground. The suicide attacks marked the disappearance of the sacrificed "martyr" and the emergence of the victorious "martyr".

Suicide bombers and suicide backers: the evolution of supply and demand

The Islamist movements, Hamas and Islamic Jihad, inaugurated in 1994 a new combat tactic against Israel by launching suicide operations into the very heart of Israeli cities. The Palestinian Authority, which was counting on the continuation of negotiations to have Palestine's sovereignty recognized, was in a difficult position. A good number of Palestinians still adhered, despite the doubts that assailed them and the setbacks they had known, to the principle of peace talks with the Israelis, and thus criticized the Islamists' initiative. Nonetheless, as the goal of Palestinian sovereignty seemed hardly to come any closer and the outcome itself became uncertain, support for the peace process waned.

When the Camp David summit meeting that brought together Bill Clinton, Yasser Arafat and Ehud Barak failed, many Palestinians became convinced that the Israeli government was not prepared to grant them their rights as a nation. Engagement in combat against the Israelis once again became the leading option. The start of the Al-Aqsa Intifada in September 2000 spelled the end of the Oslo Accords that were as good as clinically dead. Gradually the Tsahal reoccupied parts of the Territories that had become autonomous, set up blockades around the Palestinian enclaves and instituted highly repressive measures.

During both of these two periods suicide attacks were launched against Israeli civilians. Nonetheless, rather than consider these acts of violence as part of a continuum, it is important to identify the variations in the justifications given by their authors of these attacks, to trace the emergence of new types of suicide bombers and to measure the evolution of Palestinian public opinion.

1994-1999: terrorist attacks as a minority strategy. The Palestinian Islamists called for a *jihad* as soon as the peace agreement with Israel was signed in 1993, accusing the negotiators of having treasonably sold out the fundamental rights of the Palestinian people. Judging Yasser Arafat and his collaborators to be incapable of fulfilling national aspirations, Hamas claimed to represent a force capable of accomplishing the Islamic, national mission. In addition Hamas considered that the Palestinian Authority was powerless to protect its people against the operations instigated by the Israeli secret services. The desire to avenge the Palestinian deaths was a leading motivation for the perpetrators of suicide attacks. Most of these attacks were presented as responses to the disappearance of Palestinian civilians during Israeli Army operations in the territories or the elimination of political or military leaders of Islamic groups in the autonomous Territories or abroad.

The transition to radical violence decided by Hamas can be considered as the result of its leaders' decision to play a leading role in the political arena. Having been kept out of the peace negotiations, the Islamist movement was determined to break the exclusive relationship between the Palestinian Authority and the Israeli government. By attacking the Israeli population Hamas intended to prove its capacity to deal the enemy blows. Simultaneously, certain Hamas representatives were elaborating the criteria for a truce, and their declarations on occasion suggested a politically realistic approach.[14] Hamas attempted to gain recognition within the nation as the sole legitimate heir to the Intifada, taking on its national aspirations and moral values as part of the Hamas programme. On the one hand the Islamist leaders decried the "defeatist" pragmatism of Fatah and its collaborators, substituting in its place a mythic vision of Palestine "from the river to the sea". In this context they were quick to point to the shortcomings of the peace agreement, in particular the maintenance of Jewish settlements, the splitting up of the autonomous Territories and the abandonment of the refugee question. On the other hand, Hamas condemned the moral decline that had accompanied the setting up of the Authority within the Territories and the arrival of Palestinians from abroad. Criticizing the liberalization of social mores (timid though it was) while at the same time attacking the nepotism and corruption of the members of the newly installed administration, Hamas militants claimed that they alone remained true to the ideal of a political community united in its respect for religious principle and national aspiration.

The young militants of the Hamas movement were distressed in particular by the changes that came about when the Palestinian Authority took over. The fact that the Palestinian Authority claimed to bear exclusive responsibility for managing the nation's destiny and consented to a certain number of Israeli demands, especially in security matters, profoundly shocked the young Islamist *shebab*. The struggle against the Jewish state had been encouraged during the Intifada of 1987-93, and the combat had been a source of prestige; but now it was to be scorned and even penalized, and the militants and leaders of Hamas were to bear the brunt. For the activists that had taken part in the Intifada the prospect of landing up in a Palestinian jail, held and interrogated by their compatriots, was intolerable. The youngest among them, formed according to the moral order prevailing during the uprising, were amazed to discover the way their compatriots returning from Tunisia, Algiers or Beirut behaved. Their training had taught them to equate moral rigour with patriotic sentiment; relaxed moral standards were tantamount to national treason. In the Gaza Strip in particular the young Hamas members were offended by the sight of the women strolling about bareheaded, and they condemned the newcomers' taste for entertainment and alcohol. Stirred up by the speeches of their leaders, the Islamist *shebab* expressed their rejection of the peace agreements that "sold off Palestine", and denounced those in power who "served Israeli interests" and were incapable of contributing to the moral and religious values of the national community. The call to volunteer for suicide missions, increasingly heeded by the young militants of the Islamist movements, was reinforced by their indignation. Staging a suicide attack on Israel was a means of reaffirming true national objectives. Self-sacrifice for the sake of the community was considered as an act of purification that opened the way to the cleansing of a society that was fast becoming permissive and was giving up on the ideal of winning back its rights. The nationalist, moral, and religious dimensions came together in these acts committed in the name of the "*jihad*". Religion served as a moral guarantee of violence. The certainty that it was a duty and the prospect of attaining a state of bliss and beatitude in the next world were factors underlying the readiness to engage in this type of operation.

The following text, written by a suicide bomber, bears witness to the sense of disappointment that he experienced as a member of his society and his intention to incite others to accompany him in his religious and nationalist quest:

"The encounter with God is better and more precious than this life. I swear, by God, that the greatest paradise is beyond this earth's sky, for life today is but frivolous distraction and seeking after money. [...] A Jihad attack, launched by a combatant whose heart is full of faith and love for his country, frightens the arrogant and upsets their certitudes. The cry of "no" in the face of the enemy is a clear sign and will suffice for the day of victory. The battle is the concern of all, so do not remain in passive expectation of tomorrow."[15]

Ideological preparation and membership in a militant network are, in such cases, decisive factors. The leaders of the Islamist movements pay great attention to the selection of candidates and let it be known that on occasion they refuse *shebab* whom they consider as insufficiently mature to carry out such acts. They insist on the importance of the candidate's religious development. The suicide bomber only receives his operational instructions when his superiors consider that his faith is sufficiently steadfast and his moral outlook solid enough to go through with his mission. Nasra Hassan has shown the role played by the candidate's political entourage as the time draws near for the suicide attack he is to perform: those close to him keep up or rekindle his determination by evoking the rewards that await him in the next world.[16]

Hamas members have also stressed that rigorous discipline and strict respect for orders are characteristics of the movement. However, the Islamists on occasion lose control over their troops. After the assassination of Yahya Ayache by the Israeli intelligence services in January 1996, an armed cell was formed that decide to avenge the death of the "engineer". The group, motivated by the desire for revenge, instituted a campaign of extreme violence by launching five suicide attacks in the heart of Israeli cities. Its aim was also to defy Israel, and demonstrate its capacity to deal murderous blows despite the fact that the Territories had been sealed off. Hamas leaders in the Gaza Strip disavowed these acts and called for an end to the violence. This episode demonstrates the split that can occur between the strategy established by the movements' leaders and the radicalism of some of the militants.

At the time the majority of Palestinians repudiated the attacks. However, opinion fluctuated between 1994 and 2003 according to the degree of optimism concerning the peace process and its chances of success. Between June 1995 and June 1999, 20-30% of Palestinians backed the suicide attacks on Israel.[17] Roughly one quarter of the population approved of this recourse to violence and remained ambiguous in their attitude to the death of Israeli civilians. Frequently they condemned such acts in the abstract, but at the same time their thirst for vengeance or a sense of injustice led them to sympathize with the young suicide bombers. Moreover, Palestinian society took a negative view of the conflict between those in power and the Islamist opposition. Thus Hamas itself was often decried as a troublemaker, guilty of sapping national unity, and on this basis its attacks on the Israeli population came in for criticism. In addition the inhabitants of the Territories bore the consequences of the Islamist violence; the sealing of the borders by Israel paralyzed economic activity and impoverished them.

The Al-Aqsa Intifada: an impossible struggle. As the peace process got progressively bogged down, the Palestinian population concluded that Israel had deceived them. Once the failure of the negotiations became obvious, the revolt that had been smouldering in the Territories for several months broke out in the autumn of 2000. Despite a certain number of similarities with the movement begun in December 1987, the nature of the combat was basically different. Scenes of stone throwing were repeated, but for the most part the *shebab* were unable to make use of their former methods. The Israeli defences had been withdrawn, rendering the traditional techniques of civil disobedience impracticable. Now that the population of the West Bank and the Gaza Strip were autonomous there was no longer any direct contact with Israeli nerve centres. The leaders of the Palestinian Authority served as the interface with Israel or acted as administrators.

From 2001 on the massive return of Israeli military forces in the Territories ignited confrontation; the test of wills was almost immediately translated into military terms. The sealing off of the West Bank and the Gaza Strip, and the barriers set up within the area, made it impossible to travel between towns and rendered some villages inaccessible. The territorial controls were a severe handicap for the Palestinians, making the elaboration of any sort of strategy particularly difficult. Intellectuals called for the organization of non-violent forms of struggle, but they were hard put to specify how this could be achieved. Aside from the question of whether or not such tactics were possible, the *shebab* had no intention of participating in civil resistance campaigns. The conclusion that the only language that the Israelis understood was the language of force was gaining ground in the West Bank and the Gaza Strip.

Given the close quarters in which the combat was to be waged, guerrilla techniques were virtually impossible to put into practice.

Aside from a handful of successful operations, the *shebab* who attacked the settlers or the Israeli soldiers almost always missed their targets, and often endangered the lives of their fellow citizens.[18] Compared to the Israeli Army's military capacity, the Palestinians' arsenal was pathetic.

The increase in the number of suicide attacks from 2000 on, some of them the work of Fatah, can be explained in part as the result of the failure of other means of struggle. The organizers of the attacks saw in them a means of reducing the imbalance between the Palestinian combatants and the Israeli Army, with the idea that the latter's structural superiority could in this way be overcome. Given the impossibility for their troops to engage in "legitimate" violence, the alternative was to steer them towards radical forms of combat. A suicide attack does not require much in the way of material preparation; it necessitates a certain *savoir-faire* and a shrewd sense of how to elude the vigilance of the Israeli soldiers and policemen, as well as minute attention to the preparatory details which involve only a few people. Success depends for the most part on the determination of the perpetrator, on his technical astuteness and psychological self-control throughout the various steps of the process: acquiring the explosives, crossing the Green Line illegally, dressing and behaving in such a way as to avoid arousing the Israelis' suspicions, choosing the target and deciding on the best time to set off the explosives. The recourse to terrorist methods brings results for the Palestinian combatant that he could never hope to achieve by classic guerrilla tactics: a significant number of casualties and a profound psychological blow against the enemy. The essential purpose of the attack was to destabilize the opponent.

The recourse to violence was a result of the narrowing of the range of choices open to combatants against the Israeli occupation, and of Palestinian society's inability to find other means of action. The impossibility of acting in a more effective manner and the resulting sense of frustration are frequently evoked by young and old Palestinians alike. Even if the struggle against the Jewish state is considered a basic principle, Palestinian society is not convinced of the effectiveness of the methods chosen by the *shebab* who target the Israeli soldiers and the settlers in the Territories. Paradoxically, it is the sense of having failed vis-à-vis Israel that pushes certain Palestinians to adopt extreme violence. As individuals, it is virtually impossible for Palestinian youths to make plans for the future or even give any direction to their lives. It is hardly feasible for them to envisage a programme of university studies or a professional career since funds are lacking and the constraints placed on movement within the Palestinian Territories and on going abroad are even more of an obstacle. The difficulties they encounter in their personal development keep them from envisaging an emotionally satisfying life in marriage and family. The Israeli repression weighs on the daily existence of the inhabitants of the West Bank and the Gaza Strip; in a deeper sense the occupation moulds their state of mind. Thus the *shebab* have the impression of being robbed of all choice in their lives. Paradoxically, it is the planning for death, a death that will deal the enemy a decisive blow, that gives them once again a sense of initiative, devastating their opponents by their act and by the same token giving a sense to their existence. The suicide bomber overcomes his powerlessness and the powerlessness of his community in assuming his destined role of hero "martyr".[19] The foreseeable repercussions of the suicide attack in terms of loss of human life, the psychological impact, and the posthumous prestige he is sure to enjoy constitute the suicide bomber's legacy.

The new suicide bombers and Fatah's change of attitude. A turning point occurred early in 2002: the Al-Aqsa Martyr Brigades, an armed group claiming to be associated with the Fatah that had sprung up during the new Intifada, began to imitate the methods of the Islamists, perpetrating suicide attacks against Israeli civilians. They thus distanced themselves from the policies of their leaders who had laid down the rules to be followed; Fatah chiefs had in effect designated the soldiers and settlers in the West Bank and the Gaza Strip as the only legitimate targets. The Israeli repression had reached such a pitch that rank and file Fatah members became more radical and no longer felt bound by party instructions.[20]

This situation came about because of the lack of a command structure that could direct and organize the revolt against Israel. The presence of the Palestinian Authority was an obstacle that prevented the formation of an alternative leadership. Even if Yasser Arafat derived some benefit from anti-Israeli violence during the first few months of the Intifada, he could not take charge of it, as he hoped to keep, or regain, his place as a key figure on the international scene, which would not have been possible had he acted as a warlord. One cannot exclude the possibility that the Palestinian President did send instructions to Fatah militants who were engaged in operations and did finance certain military groups; however, a significant number of *shebab* who were associated with Fatah paid little attention to the their leaders' instructions and policies, taking advantage of the absence of a coordinating structure. In addition, the fact that the Territories were dispersed and their inhabitants isolated contributed to the multiplication of separate groups cut off from each other. The gangs engaged in the struggle against Israel were subject to the conditions that prevailed in their particular sectors. The *shebab* gained a certain freedom of action as a result, and they had no intention of relinquishing their autonomy. Their organization was based, even more than in the past, on neighbourhood connections and affective ties. The loss of one member of the group could sometimes set off a violent reaction, while analysis of the political and military context is a secondary concern.

Hence decisions that were supposed to be binding on all the military units were difficult to negotiate; there were many parties involved, and the situation could vary from one group to the next. A truce declaration required that all the protagonists should be contacted. The maintenance of a truce was only possible when none of the cells that had the capacity to act was subject to Israeli army repression; if the army intervened it could set off a counterattack.

The increase in the number of suicide attacks is closely related to the evolution of supply and demand in terms of national mobilization. On the one hand, the traditional methods which Fatah had used previously no longer paid off. These methods confined Fatah to the role of a victim that had not even managed to win significant international support. With the increasingly violent forays of the Israeli Army and its increasingly violent tactics, the imbalance between the two parties grew. The dwindling number of tactical choices open to Fatah put it at a disadvantage compared to the "successes" of the Islamist militants who carried out their lethal operations. Fatah members intended to remain in the front ranks of leadership, but they were concerned lest more effective combatants eclipse them. Extreme violence was seen as a way of obliging the enemy to curb the use of force.

Fatah's conversion to radical modes of operation and its recourse to religious rhetoric should not, however, be interpreted as an ideological transformation of the organization. It stems rather from decisions taken by individual militants subjected to extreme conditions. The shift in tactics also reflected the evolution of Palestinian public opinion, which backed the decision to use violence against Israeli civilians, even if victory no longer appeared possible. For a certain category of the young who applied as candidates for suicide attacks it was no doubt easier to receive Fatah's endorsement. Some Hamas spokesmen asserted that the number of candidates for suicide operations had increased to the point that their organization could not handle all of them. The training Hamas insisted on, and its determination to give importance to the religious dimension, resulted in a stricter selection process. Hamas continues to be the leading organizer of attacks against Israel, but Fatah, responsible for roughly one quarter of the suicide attacks since 2002, recruits from a wider range of candidates. The three girls who blew themselves up in the heart of Israeli cities were identified with the Al-Aqsa Martyr Brigades. It seems as well that Fatah armed groups tend to send younger *shebab* out on missions.

The "younger brothers" generation : socialisation through violence. Pénélope Larzillière has remarked that with the Al-Aqsa Intifada, the candidates for suicide attacks came from a wider range of backgrounds, and that it is impossible today to define their "sociological profile".[21] Despite this greater heterogeneity, Avishai Margalit has pointed out that the great majority of suicide bombers are young single men between 17 and 28 years old, and that half of them come from the refugee camps.[22]

Several factors can serve to explain the fact that these "younger brothers" are ready to turn themselves into human bombs. Unlike their elders they know little of politics and remain outside party structures. The setting up of the first Intifada was the result of the training of the rank and file by the political organizations in the 1970s and 1980s; these organizations are far less effective in the context of Palestinian autonomy. The young also stay away from such organizations because they hesitate to become engaged in political infighting. The tensions between the Islamist movement and the Palestinian Authority are all the more destabilizing for the population and especially for the young since they undermine the myth of Palestinian unanimity. The "younger brothers" consider the conflicts between the representatives of the different political parties as sterile debates; therefore they refuse to choose between the various strategies that are proposed. By standing aside, this generation is deprived of a process of political socialization.

Moreover those in the 16-25 age bracket express themselves in radical terms, especially in regard to the Israelis. In their eyes, their adversaries are those who have come to occupy their land: the soldiers or the settlers. Their elders had the opportunity to meet Israelis in other circumstances: they might have found employment on the other side of the Green Line when crossing over was entirely possible. Deprived of any contact with their adversary, the youngest Palestinians develop a quasi-fantasized relationship with a political enemy that they have difficulty in imagining in human terms. Thus it is easier for them to entertain the prospect of sending Israeli civilians to their deaths.

To transform oneself into a suicide bomber is a way of short-circuiting political mediation and escaping individual and collective powerlessness by a personal act of war against the enemy. While this phenomenon is an indication of collective distress, it is also part of the process of individualization and self-affirmation within Palestinian society.

Is the suicide attack strategy a failure?

The aim of terrorizing the Israelis, of dealing them sufficiently massive blows for them to force their government to give up repression and settlement, has up to now been a failure. The suicide attacks have reinforced radical tendencies in Israeli public opinion; to a great extent the Israelis have approved the decisions taken by their leaders in political and security matters. A majority of them are now convinced that it is impossible to live with the Palestinians and that it will be difficult to reach a peace agreement with them. The Israeli left felt betrayed by Yasser Arafat's attitude at Camp David, considering that the aged Palestinian leader had obstinately refused the "generous offers" made for the first time by Ehud Barak. There is little disagreement on this issue in Israel.[23]

Moreover, the decision to attack civilians has tarnished the reputation of the Palestinians in international terms. The continuation of suicide attacks after the events of September 11, 2001 confirmed the illegitimacy of such acts in the eyes of Western public opinion. Ariel Sharon proved himself most astute in deriving advantage from the international context by convincing the American government that Yasser Arafat and Osama Bin Laden were equivalent and that the suicide attacks launched against Israeli civilians by Palestinian militants were no different from Al-Qaida's attacks on the United States. The Palestinian Islamist organizations, aware of the danger, decreed a moratorium on suicide operations; a few months later, the Al-Aqsa Martyr Brigades also decided to abandon such attacks — at least provisionally. In fact the Palestinians have not ceased to call on the world to witness the injustice of which they are the victims. Their hesitations about the type of struggle to wage reveal the ambiguities of their situation and the weakness of their strategy.

3

KASHMIRI SUICIDE BOMBERS:
'MARTYRS' OF A LOST CAUSE

Amélie Blom

In 1993, several weeks after a young tailor's apprentice from Karachi had disappeared, his family learned that he was in the Kashmir Valley where, as he put it, he hoped "to have his head cut off by the Hindu dogs for the salvation of Islam."[1] He was the first "martyr" of the Lashkar-i-Tayyeba (the Army of the Pure), the largest Jihadist organization based in Pakistan. In 2000, it was the father of a secondary school student from Srinagar who was astonished to discover that his son had just driven a car crammed full of explosives into the headquarters of the 15th Indian army corps. He was the very first Kashmiri to turn himself into a human bomb, at the instigation of the Jaish-i-Muhammad (the Army of Muhammad, another Jihadist organization based in Pakistan). These two were among the fifteen thousand young people[2] who have died in Kashmir since 1993. That is when this unheard-of phenomenon – the emergence of "martyrs" as the favoured strategy in the armed struggle, and as a political and social fact of life – began to develop within the secessionist rebellion in this Indian province and within the society of neighbouring Pakistan.

The "suicide attacks", as Indian authorities began calling them in 1999,[3] are part of a movement which, throughout the second half of the 1990s, built up the figure of the "martyr" – a combatant whose death was so probable that it was prepared for, desired, and above all regarded as sacred. The ten or so armed "Jihadist" groups from which they grew had no monopoly on the term "martyr" (*shahid*), used by the Pakistani army and non-Islamist Kashmiri organizations alike. But they were the only ones who used it as a strategy to prepare young people to die in the "earthly paradise" of Kashmir, as it is conceived in the Pakistani national imagination (its lakes lined with plane trees decorate hundreds of taxi scooters in Lahore). They have played such a crucial role that, in contrast to the case of Palestine, no "martyrdom operations" in Kashmir are carried out individually.[4]

These organizations grew stronger owing to the receptivity of Kashmiri society, which had witnessed the gradual failure of "ethnic" Kashmiri nationalism over the previous ten years. In Pakistan, on the other hand, their ability to recruit future "martyrs" among young people was achieved through the progressive alteration of a completely different ideological project – the militaristic nationalism of a state that had been developing into an "Islamic Leviathan" since the late 1970s.[5] These two complementary dynamics are the subject of this chapter.

From a war for national liberation to Islamist guerrilla warfare

Today, the mobilization for secession in Kashmir, which began in the 1920s, is driven by groups with contradictory options (autonomy, independence, union with Pakistan). Since 1993 they have been represented by the All Parties Hurriyat Conference (APHC), which stands against both the Indian federal government and the National Congress Party that has run Kashmir for the past 27 years. In the mid-sixties, sporadic armed attacks were launched by the Jammu and Kashmir Liberation Front (JKLF), a nationalist force favouring independence for the reunited territory of the former princely state. Popular resentment was transformed into an armed rebellion by New Delhi's total abandonment of the political autonomy initially granted (and, in effect, of the referendum for self-determination provided for in UN resolutions since 1948); and above all by the rigged elections in 1987 (assuring the victory of the National Congress Party, which gave up defending the autonomist card it had once supported). Then, hundreds of young Muslims – feeling that they were not integrated into the Indian state[6] and were no longer permitted to express themselves through legal channels – went to Pakistan, to the JKLF's training camps.

At that time the Islamic side of the rebellion occupied a marginal place in JKLF rhetoric, as with the Palestinian PLO and the Algerian FLN. The situation changed in 1990. Worried about the ricochet effect of its pro-independence mobilization in the part of Kashmir it controlled, Pakistan began pushing and supporting another group, Hizb ul-Mujahidin, which advocated Kashmir's unification with Pakistan. This *"mujahidin* party", run by an Islamist candidate (of the Jamaat-i-Islami) deprived of victory in the 1987 elections, was the first to make Islamism — in whose name it "eliminated" a number of JKLF officers — one of the issues in the secessionist struggle. The Islamization of the guerrilla forces began to increase in 1993-94. Armed groups proliferated — they numbered over one hundred in 1992, drawn by Pakistani funds and the potential for extortion. Moreover, the "renegade" groups trained by the Indian Army started retaliating against the families of Hizb militants. This led Pakistan to introduce movements into the struggle that were operating exclusively within its own borders and, until then, had been active only in Afghanistan.[7] Consequently, the interaction between the Pakistani state and the Jihadist groups took an unusual turn when the former encouraged the development within its own territory of irregular armies with an ideological motivation (there were no mere mercenaries), to which it assigned aggressive guerrilla actions, and which recruited within its own society and among its neighbours.

These "guest *mujahidin*" (as Hizb calls them) had the advantage of more easily avoiding retaliation. The goal was also to "purge" the re-

bellion of its small criminal element. Their purpose was to save the irredentist project of uniting Kashmir with Pakistan from being further
discredited (their orders, enforced in the early days, were not to force
people to house, feed or finance the combatants). The growing effi-
ciency of the Indian counter-insurrection (which made imprisonment
or death an increasingly likely end) was gradually driving the Jihadists
to establish an ideological framework in which "martyrdom" was no
longer simply an element of combat rhetoric, but its motivating force.
Naturally, Muslim society in the Valley was already accustomed to the
politicization of the idea of *shahadat* (martyrdom),[8] but until then its
purpose had been the Kashmiri nationalist struggle, of which it was
simply an unfortunate consequence. From 1993 to 1999, the mobilization in favour of "martyrdom" was aimed above all at preparing
militants to die, as they were being increasingly surrounded, and to
confront the Indian army directly in ambushes.

The first time the word "suicide" was used to describe an attack
was on 13 July 1999, when the Indo-Pakistani war was in full swing.
In fact, it was only a failed attempt to kidnap some officers; but the
term was established then, during the media war the Indian government waged successfully against Pakistan. Lashkar, which claimed
responsibility for it, described it as a *fedayeen* action (*fedayeen* = "those
who sacrifice themselves" for a cause). This tactic consisted in taking
into a military camp or a police station a small group of militants who
fired as long as they could on the greatest possible number of people.[9]
Aware of the shame aroused by suicide in the Islamic faith, it declared
that, in contrast to the Palestinian "suicide attacks", its "*fedayeen* always
have a chance of surviving. Moreover, 70% have survived."[10] But the
risks were such that the combatants' anticipation of their death was
indeed the core of the strategy, as the organization acknowledged
elsewhere.[11] Jaish-i-Muhammad is the only organization since 2000 to
have claimed responsibility for true "suicide attacks" (mostly carried
out by young recruits in India). This organization with dubious origins

belongs to an Islamist movement which the Pakistani government has
always had a very hard time controlling.

Mourning ethnic nationalism and self-sacrifice

The mobilization of candidates for "martyrdom" appeared belatedly in
the history of Kashmiri secessionism - at the end of over fifty years of
the separatist movement and five years of armed insurrection. It arose
over the long term from the fact that the Pakistani government had
been subcontracting the war to irregular forces since its creation in
1947, as well as from the increasingly repressive strategies carried out
by the Indian government. But how did Kashmir come to be an object
of a phantasmagorical death-wish for thousands of young militants
facing an Indian army with a hundred times more men? While Indian
propaganda systematically spoke of "foreign terrorists", there were in
fact a very high number of Kashmiri recruits.[12] 35,000 of them were
arrested at the LOC[13] between 1990 and 1996 (1,700 more crossed it
in 2001) – far from negligible in proportion to the million and a half
young Muslims aged 15 to 25 in Jammu and Kashmir. Despite the difficulty of obtaining information about these recruits, whose families
always affirm they know nothing about their activities from fear of
retaliation, we can put forward some hypotheses about their principal
motivations.

The most striking thing at first is the intensely personal nature of
the fight. "My father was made a *shahid* because he was with Jamaat-
i-Islami, so I'm going to train in Pakistan," proclaims a little boy in a
Hizb propaganda video.[14] The very first Kashmiri "human bomb" was
also the son of a member of this party, which has lost over 2,000 of
its members at the hands of Indian security forces.[15] It is no longer a
matter, as it was at the beginning of the rebellion, of risking one's life
in the name of a new collective future, but rather of "paying back" a
close relation's death, imprisonment or suffering. This logic of revenge goes beyond Islamist party members. One young man, while
still at university, joined the ranks of Hizb after being arrested and, ac-

cording to the organization, tortured by the police for having started a demonstration in his village against an Indian member of parliament.[16] Another, who had gone to the best private (Christian) school in Srinagar, suddenly left the United States, where he was training to be an airline pilot, and went to a camp in Pakistan to prepare to die "as a 'martyr'". After his death, one member of the family attributed his act to a need to "overcome the contradiction" between his own success and his growing feelings of guilt at being powerless "to serve Islam", whereas his best friend had been killed by the Indian army.[17] The dynamics of personal revenge also determined the commitment of the sons of Kashmiri refugees who came to Pakistan in 1947, such as the young man from Lashkar who became a *shahid* in the very district where his mother constantly spoke of her dreams of an impossible return. Indeed, she referred to his "martyrdom" as an "atonement" for her suffering.

"Martyrdom" is evoked by the Kashmiris as an individual act dissociated from any political project. The phenomenon can be explained through the peculiar evolution in the secessionist rebellion. Indeed, there is a considerable gap between the former conviction that independence was to be soon won with guns – the dominant feeling in the early nineties – and the opinion constantly expressed by young people in Srinagar today that "the Indians will never leave Kashmir".[18] Death as a "martyr" can be seen as the ultimate phase in their sentiment that the national struggle has been totally defeated. It is felt even more cruelly because there is no Kashmiri political force left to embody their hopes for political change. The JKLF, like all the other non-religious armed groups, had to give up armed struggle in 1994. The APHC still echoes a genuinely Kashmiri nationalism; but it has been entirely discredited through in-fighting and the inability to have an effective dialogue with New Delhi. Finally, Hizb, the only mainly Kashmiri armed group that is still active, denies the existence of a "Kashmiri nation", keeping its struggle exclusively within the framework of irredentist nationalism in Pakistan where most of its leadership is based.

Yet this political void has not weakened the desire for independence,[19] nowadays mainly fuelled by the appalling humanitarian situation.[20] All options are closed to these young people, who no longer believe in the possibility of living other than as "second-class citizens in India, where we are treated as either Pakistani agents or mere subjects." For this reason, they support Jihadist practices but not Jihadist ideology ("I wouldn't like to see Kashmir run by Hizb, Lashkar or Jaish, but who else fights against the army? Who else is interested in us?" said one girl[21]). Some of the young people, compared locally to the Palestinian Intifada, were galvanized recently – in a disorganized fashion – to defy the curfew and throw stones at soldiers. Mocking them, they asked to be given back the bodies of Lashkar militants and attended the funeral of a Pakistani commander of Jaish-i-Muhammad (as in August 2003 in Srinagar).

The receptivity shown to the Jihadists can be explained by the failure of Kashmiri ethnic nationalism in the context of total impunity in which Indian security forces have operated. But the relentless pursuit of suicide comes more specifically from the insoluble paradoxes of the Jihadist guerrilla war itself. The idea that the war's prohibitive cost will force the Indian army to leave is no longer a convincing argument for anyone. One Lashkar leader acknowledged it implicitly by stating that the main victory obtained after ten years of *jihad* was the creation of "a generation of Kashmiris" who "have seen their father or mother become a *shahid* before their very eyes" and will be motivated to become the future "martyrs,"[22] in other words, for having prompted a situation where the proliferation of civilian casualties is inevitable. Less cynically, a Hizb militant stated that "it's hard to liberate Kashmir. If we succeed, we shall have been victorious in this world and in the Beyond, and if we don't succeed but become 'martyrs', then we shall still be victorious in the Beyond." Through "martyrdom", as Larzillière observed, defeat is transformed into victory by being shifted to the immeasurable temporality of the sacred.[23]

Yet there is another dimension beyond the strategic function of dying as a "martyr" that constitutes its singularity – its purifying power which grows out of a different dynamic. This aspect is very difficult to analyze in the absence of a micro-sociological study of the future "martyr", which alone would allow us to see how his psychology and vision of the world are shaped by the social and political environment. One could advance the hypothesis that such expiatory quests should be understood in the context of the "degeneration" of the secessionist struggle into a process of self-destruction. At war with India and undermined by fear, suspicion, widespread extortion and denunciation, Muslim society in northern Kashmir is also at war with itself; it is "totally schizophrenic" according to a teacher in Srinagar ("You never know who your colleague or neighbour could be. An Indian agent? A militant?"). Today it is caught in the crossfire of agents of repression who blend in more and more with the local population ("renegades", informers, village militias) and Jihadists whose *Diktats* about people's personal lives have intensified considerably in recent years. Moreover, the fratricidal war between the secessionist forces has been covered up by a "layer of silence and lies that hold India and Pakistan solely responsible for the failure of the freedom movement."[24] An initial interpretation might see the "martyr" contrasting the purity of his choice to die with the "Hindu dog", as stated in the Jihadist rhetoric. But his death ultimately speaks to the internal evils which in the end have dashed the hopes of creating a nation that is Kashmiri by virtue of being Muslim (an ambiguous stance already present in the JKLF's nationalism).

Manufacturing "martyrs" and the failure of praetorian Islamic nationalism in Pakistan

What factors within the dissimilar context of Pakistan have prompted the emergence of this "martyr" phenomenon? As in the case of Kashmir, sources are a problem when trying to analyze the phenomenon (wills left by the "martyrs" and testimonials from their families are, most of the time, written by Jihadist propagandists, or simply made up).[25] Yet strong enough differences sometimes emerge from these stereotypical discourses to reveal individual thoughts. The "martyrs" are young (aged 16-23), and from large families (7-10 children). They are poor or from the lower middle class (the fathers are hired hands, bicycle repairmen or migrant workers in the Gulf) and are from the outskirts of large industrial cities like Faisalabad. They have left school as teenagers and are most often single. But that description corresponds to millions of young Pakistanis whose socio-economic frustration would never drive them to voluntarily be killed in Kashmir. So there is no "typical sociological profile" to fit candidates for "martyrdom". We must therefore examine the individual paths that lead people to join Jihadist organizations. The three ideal types identified by Khosrokhavar for the Bassidji[26] ("playful", "opportunist" and "martyropath") provide a clue that is all the more useful in that it also helps to understand the originality of the process of manufacturing "martyrs" in which Jihadist organizations are involved in Pakistan.

A large number of Pakistani teenagers join the "*jihad*" (a term often associated with the word *shoq*, evoking a favourite pastime) drawn by the promise of thrills and romantic "martial camaraderie" intensified by Jihadist chants.[27] "An eagle unfolding his wings," the "*mujahid*" is all the more thirsty for individual autonomy because of overcrowded living conditions and postponed marriages, making family pressures increasingly unbearable. He also has a "hip" image – often underestimated. The success of the deceptively titled film *In Your Love* (*Tere pyar main*) is a case in point. The film is about the transformation of a young adman from Lahore into an intrepid Hizb militant (who goes off to liberate his "Kashmiri brothers" after a horrible Indian conspiracy against his fiancée!). "Neither cricket stars nor movie stars, but Islamic *mujahidin*," Lashkar banners proclaimed at an event organized in Lahore in 2001. The *mujahidin* claim to "hate fashion", yet the two thousand recruits present at this event were all wearing Rambo-style "*mujahidin* camouflage (*sic*)," or baseball caps sporting the name of their organization; but they wore them over a *shalwar* (traditional trousers) rolled up over the ankles, according to a custom attributed to the Prophet. The *mujahid* look is only one example of the crossover between modernity and tradition[28] proudly accepted by these "playful" types. They live near "modern" cities with no access to the consumer goods enjoyed only by the Westernized elite, who in fact look for "fulfilment" more in life than in death.

"Opportunists" too are initially looking for a break here on earth rather than in death. The logic at work is often farcical, like the young man who succeeded in stealing funds from a Jihadist organization to open his own electronics shop.[29] Although initially disconcerting, the constant economic references in Jihadist literature provide an insight into this material motivation: Lashkar recruits are described as "*jihad* contract workers" who "make deals", "bargain with God", and bring in enough "profit" and "income" to keep their homes running. Moreover, Lashkar students learn that "their future profession as *mujahidin* will be in high demand over the next millennium";[30] so it is not surprising to read that a young man proudly displays his "*mujahidin* camouflage" in front of his father as if it were his work uniform, exclaiming "that's how we operate in enemy territory!" The organization also attracts young people with a different kind of opportunism. Those who have already fallen into delinquency are fleeing arrest or gangland killings (their mothers often speak of their "bad habits" – theft in particular). "Some have fought with a rival family or committed murder," confirmed one Hizb militant, adding that "others simply want to learn how to use a gun and become a dacoït [gangster]."[31]

Some young people are driven by truly "martyropath" impulses, like the sons of officers of Jihadist organizations and Islamist parties. Trained from a very young age to believe that dying as a "martyr" is sacred, they could not imagine a different kind of future; some of them spent their childhood holidays rock climbing with "*mujahidin*" in the mountains of Azad Kashmir, others were trained in Lashkar schools. Alongside them are other young "martyropaths" for whom life has lost any appeal or meaning, like the "martyrs" whose mothers speak of their children's extreme loneliness and depression ("without any friends", "came into the world and left it like a blank page", "incapable of holding down a steady job"). One militant wrote to his father, a farmer, that "a tree planted by a gardener in the hope of enjoying its fruit will grant him even better fruits in the Beyond if he is sacrificed on God's Path. Dear father, I couldn't live up to your expectations, but that sadness will vanish in the Beyond." Unable to straighten out his painful personal situation, the future "martyr" turns things around through his own death; a death as a "martyr" valued in the existing belief system. The same is true for one young drug addict, sent to a Jihadist camp as a substitute for drug rehab by his mother who was thrilled that "the local kids have stopped calling him *jehaz* [high] and now call him *mujahid*."

The main thrust of the Jihadist organizations' propaganda is to swell the ranks of the small but determined group of "martyropaths" to whom Jihadism appeals – not as a game (for the "playful") or a refuge (for the "opportunists"), but rather through its apocalyptic dimension.[32] It is above all an undertaking designed to manufacture "martyropaths" who accept their lot. That purpose is fulfilled through phantasmagorical stories of military victories – painting an enticing but very unlikely picture of returning to Kashmir as a *ghazi* (one who returns from battle as a victor) – and above all through long descriptions of post-"martyrdom". Indeed the parents, as well as the militants – whose testimonies all express the fear that "God will not accept" their *shahadat*, because of past sins or residual doubts about the legitimacy of their violent acts – must be convinced they will inevitably be granted "martyr" status. Hence the stories of "martyrs" forbidding their mothers to mourn them ("You shouldn't cry over a *shahid*. You should thank God!", one of them said to her weeping husband) or to organize group recitations of the Koran (praying for their souls to be at peace would deny them "martyr" status, which absolves all sins),[33] and asking them to give milk – a symbol of purity and the favourite drink of the Prophet ("the greatest *shahid* of all") – to the "brothers who bring the news" of their "martyrdom". This also explains the multiple references to the militant's presence in Paradise. That presence – which haunts the dreams of so many mothers struggling to accept the kind of loss that no ideological spin could ever make bearable[34] – is attested by the "martyr's" promise to intercede with God so that his close relatives will be taken in too (a privilege reserved in Islam for "those who have died on the path of Allah"). Finally, in the exceptional cases where the family recovers the militant's body, it becomes a pretext for demonstrating the sacred nature of his remains.[35]

In an extraordinary slip of the tongue, one Hizb militant said that "martyrdom" was "created".[36] Indeed, the figure of the "martyr" results mainly from destructuring of the primary personality and construction of a person who has no identity apart from his characterization by others. To that end, the organization carries out an intense programme of conditioning. The physically weak young person (sleep-deprived as no more than three hours' sleep is allowed) is subjected to training that favours indoctrination over physical exercise,[37] and lives cut off from the world in a camp located miles from his home. He only rarely sees his family, whom he now judges only according to his "Islamicized" morals. Family stories are full of examples of radical changes on a physical and psychological level. The process has been compared to being "bewitched" ("those Lashkar people made him breathe in the *gidar singhi* [snake charmers' talisman], and made him so devout that his heart couldn't bear to stay home any longer," said one sister). In the meantime he has been given a new name by the organization (he is no longer Imran but Abu Bakr, and he now identifies with the companions of the Prophet from the early days of Islam, the only standard by which he now interprets the present) before ultimately becoming a "number" (his "ticket to Paradise") on a waiting list to cross the LOC.

This physical, psychological and temporal relocation, which ensures the young person's depersonalization and facilitates his being killed, is supported all along by a particular strategy underpinning the Jihadist undertaking – turning the recruit away from his innermost inherited sense of religion. This is a particularly important aspect in the context of Pakistani Sunni Islam, divided into various sects that often display a lethal rivalry. Lashkar, for example, aims above all to turn the candidate for "martyrdom" into a vehicle for converting people from the mainstream Barelwi school of thought to the Ahl-i-Hadith movement.[38] The testimony of the sister of one "martyr" is a perfect example of this. Before dying in the Valley, her brother succeeded in convincing the inhabitants of his village that claims about a sacred tree were "fraudulent" by cutting it down without going blind as had been predicted by those guarding the grave of a saint over which the tree was hanging. By associating the "heroism" of the struggle against heterodox village customs with that of a young man willing to sacrifice his life to defeat "the Hindu infidels", the organization was trying to provide unquestionable proof of the superiority of its school of thought.

The creation of "martyrs" inherently serves the Jihadist movements' organizational purposes. But it could never have become a social phenomenon – the death-wish of some Pakistani youth – without the unusual political context out of which it arose: the progressive fusion of nationalism and Islamism, initially brought about not by Islamist forces but rather by the military elite. As early as the late 1950s the army began to counter community-based nationalism ("the Muslim nation") – promoted by the forces which had presided over the birth of Pakistan (the Muslim League and the bureaucracy) – with a competing image ("the army is the nation") that was in a position to establish the legitimacy of a praetorian state. But it was only under the dictatorship of General Zia ul-Haq (1977-88), during whose rule the number of Jihadist recruits swelled – and in the context of the Afghan "*jihad*" against the Soviets, encouraged by the government itself – that a third variant of official nationalism came to the fore: "the army is the Islamic nation." And yet the unprecedented Islamization of educational, judicial, penal, financial and land ownership policies underpinning this project (which no democratic government later dared to dismantle) was chiefly oriented at the most vulnerable sectors of society which the Jihadist recruits come from. Thus these sectors were also the main victims of its social and economic failure. The moral authority granted to the most conservative religious forces at the neighbourhood level, and the austerity imposed through the abusive power of censorship bodies,[39] created enormous frustration among young people. Meanwhile, the crisis in the 1980s, rampant corruption, rising unemployment and a decline in potential jobs abroad destroyed their hopes for "Islamic" social justice. Stories from the "martyrs" are like a distorting mirror of that failure. "A believer's Kalashnikov is his jewels," as Lashkar militants often say, trying to reconcile the contradiction between egalitarian Islamic rhetoric and the impossibility of social advancement. "My brother was always mad about something, but after joining the *jihad* he became very respectful of his elders and very good to the poor," said another sister. The truth of her story is less important than her message – the possibility of channelling his "rage" while being in sync with Islamic ideals (respect for elders, and charity) at a time when they are at risk due to the economic crisis. Furthermore, the Jihadist recruit goes from being a passive victim of the process of Islamization (and its failure) to an active agent by transforming himself and those around him; for *jihad* begins at home, where he forces his close relatives to "throw the television out the window", the women to respect a strict separation from the men (*purdah*) and even to get rid of family photographs.

Equally important is the inversion of social hierarchies promised by death as a "martyr". Young people from Lashkar (almost all from traditional areas of emigration to the Gulf, many of whom have fathers or brothers working there) "tear up their visas for Dubai" in favour of a "visa for Paradise".[40] This is not just because the "Zia years" of easy and cheap legal emigration to the Gulf are over. It is also because, although such migration allows them to get rich, it does not modify their status within an extremely hierarchical Pakistani society.[41] "Guys who join the *jihad* are often sick and tired of being on the side of the weak. Their family is in conflict with a *chaudhry* [Punjabi landowner] and must submit, so he wants to make people respect him through the use of weapons," said one Hizb militant.[42] That desire for respect does not always meet with success. "Our *maulwi*[43] are deceiving our youth – with long beards to hide their fat stomachs. They tell them to 'join the *jihad* to earn a salary'," said one villager from Jalo, a Punjabi town which is the birthplace of a Lashkar militant. Be that as it may, the future "martyr" can always dream of reversing all the social inequalities in death, and promise eternal virgins (wives of the chosen ones who are allowed into Paradise) to his mother exhausted from daily chores – a bevy of "daughters-in-law" to serve her like a rich woman's servants.

Yet it would be misleading to focus solely on this sacralization of social status inaccessible in the here and now. The militant does not die only as a "martyr", but also as a "hero" who has fallen in defence of his country, Pakistan, like any *shahid* from the Pakistani army. There is indeed a form of "Islamic nationalism"[44] at play here. This is demonstrated by the fact that the first organization to supply Pakistani recruits for the "Kashmir *jihad*" was the student union Jamaat-i-Islami, which had made its debut in the "patriotic" effort against Bengali secessionists and India in 1971. Moreover, Jihadist movements have taken up all the official nationalist rhetoric. The Lashkar slogan "*Pakistan ka matlab kya hai? La ilaha ila'llah*" or "What is the meaning of Pakistan? There is no god but Allah" is the same one used by the Movement for Pakistan in the forties.[45]

But the intensified official nationalist propaganda prompted a reaction in the opposite direction, which largely explains the suicidal desperation of the Islamist guerrilla forces trained by the Pakistani army. Schoolchildren may continue to learn how to hate "Hindu" India persecuting Kashmiris, glorify *shahadat* and hold forth about *jihad*,[46] but Kashmir is now a lost cause. The Pakistani army was powerless to do anything about the failure of the irredentist project (in the years 1965-71), then of the guerrilla war using Kashmiri proxies – ethnic nationalists at first (the JKLF mobilized in Azad Kashmir from 1988 to 1990), later pro-Pakistanis (when the rebellion was criminalized in 1990-93) – and finally of the Pakistani Jihadists (incapable of forcing India to negotiate since 1993). Worst of all, the army actually encouraged the Jihadist groups (particularly Lashkar, in the politically crucial province of Punjab) in order to legitimize the "infra-conventional" war in Kashmir in the eyes of the people. But the people, exhausted by this faraway and costly "cause", clearly expressed their dissatisfaction. The failure of the "Islamic Leviathan" can be seen quite distinctly in people's resistance – intense, despite generally accepted ideas[47] – to Jihadist recruitment efforts, in their negative perception of these organizations "that gobble up riyals from foreign agents, drive young people to leave school, brainwash them and then throw them into war like sacrificed sheep" (as suggested in the description of Lashkar by the repentant mother of a *shahid*), and in their notable absence from the official festivities on the Day of Solidarity for Kashmir, which only Jihadist militants now attend.

The failure of the ethnic nationalist ideological project in Kashmir, and of the praetorian Islamic nationalist one in Pakistan – as well as the abandonment of all hope of transforming the social and political order – has enabled Jihadist organizations to use the thirst for revenge, thrills, social mobility and atonement experienced by some young people for their own purposes. Putting oneself to death reverses the extremely unfavourable balance of power, not just between the group and one's enemy (or enemies) but also, and in a fundamental way, between the individual and his utopia. A comparative analysis of contemporary phenomena of eschatological violence and a micro-sociological study of the individual itineraries of the "martyrs" would enable one to question that hypothesis, which is put forward here to account only for the socio-political motivation behind the "martyrdom" phenomenon in Kashmir. Moreover, that dynamic has different repercussions in Kashmir itself than in Pakistan. In the former case, the political trap has snapped shut. While during the years 1988-93 the insurgents were supported by a social movement (those "nationalist heroes" whose mothers celebrated their departure for Pakistani camps with henna rituals), "nowadays," said one young woman from Srinagar, "we no longer know the militants and we find out afterwards that they were one of our neighbours." The ties that once united the militants with society have been broken.

This shift in the secessionist struggle can contribute to an intensification of suicidal violence in the future. In Pakistan the army took charge of the "martyr" phenomenon, thus generating a different dynamic. This enabled organizations over which it had only partial control to carry out the Islamization of society – by delegating to private armies the two legitimizing processes (Islamization and the Kashmiri cause) which had been a monopoly of the state until then – in the name of that "cause". From that point on, these organizations have developed in the opposite direction from Palestinian and Algerian Islamists. Their reasoning starts with purification and sacrifice, and ends with political struggle in the here and now, in Pakistan. A typical example is that of Lashkar, which now focuses on medical aid and education, concentrating its efforts on areas abandoned by the government – like the war previously.

4

CHECHNYA: MOVING TOWARD
ISLAMIC NATIONALISM?

Pénélope Larzillière

Between the first Russo-Chechen war of independence (1994-96) and the resumption of the conflict in 1999, the range of actions employed by the Chechens evolved, as did the intensity of Russian army operations. While ambushes against the latter have remained the Chechen combatants' principal mode of action, recent developments in the conflict have been marked by the emergence of suicide attacks. The first war ended with the signing of the Khassaviurt accord in August 1996,[1] following the serious setbacks experienced by the Russian army. A treaty was signed in 1997 prohibiting the use of force in relations between the two countries. However, the situation in an independent Chechnya turned out to be difficult. The shattered economy left between 80 and 90% of the working population jobless.[2] Russian promises of reconstruction in fact resulted in the economic isolation of Chechen territory through checkpoints set up all along the border. On the domestic scene, elections were organized in 1997. The candidates who were the most intransigent towards the Russians and who had Islamist leanings, such as Basayev[3] and Udugov (Minister of Information under President Dudayev), were outnumbered by Maskhadov, the head of the Chechen army known for his willingness to compromise and negotiate with the Russians. Yet Maskhadov had great difficulty in establishing his authority over the whole of Chechnya, with certain warlords refusing to retreat. In October 1999, Dagestani and Chechen Islamist combatants, led by Basayev, made an incursion into Dagestan to provide assistance to Wahhabi villages. In doing so, they gave the Russians an excuse to invade Chechnya again.

On the Russian side, the second war was marked by far more extensive bombings, village "sweeps", the establishment of "filtration camps", ransom-taking, etc. In addition to traditional guerrilla methods, in 2000 the Chechens began launching suicide attacks against the Russian army, as well as against the pro-Russian Chechen administration, for which Basayev generally claimed responsibility. The suicide attacks were strongly influenced by the idea of the *shahid*, or Islamic "martyr". Websites for many jihadist organizations readily portrayed Chechnya as one of the fronts where Muslims were being oppressed by *kuffar*, or "infidels", in this case Russians. The Russians immediately highlighted this state of affairs and made a direct link between such actions and Al-Qaida-style international terrorism. The suicide attacks, rejected by the people, were then presented as the result of foreign influence, i.e. the "Wahhabis". Thus arose the issue of the "Palestinization" of the conflict, officially referred to for the first time in June 2003 by FSB (ex-KGB) director Nikolai Patrushev, as well as by certain journalists such as Anna Politovskaia.[4]

But does the increase in suicide attacks in Chechnya mean the Chechen struggle has been co-opted by international jihadist movements? The theory we will develop here attempts to highlight the evolution of that struggle from nationalism to Islamic nationalism, as the discourse justifying the war is increasingly filled with religious references, while the issues at stake have remained nationalist. Such references are also historical, as they were already present during the anti-colonial struggles in the 19th century. Moreover, although the use of suicide attacks is part of the evolution towards Islamic nationalism, this increase in sacrificial violence cannot be attributed to the

Islamists alone. Indeed, the latter were very present during the first Chechen war when such actions were not employed. Other aspects must therefore be included in order to understand this change. We must be careful in our analysis in any case, as the inaccessible terrain makes it difficult to evaluate the real impact of references to martyrdom on the population and groups of combatants.

Islamism: an Islamic nationalist reinterpretation of the national struggle?

Although Islam has been present in the region since the 8th century, it was not massively established in Chechnya until the 18th, and was implanted mainly in the 19th century during the Caucasus wars.[5] The relationship between Chechen Islam and the anti-colonial wars constitutes an important point in understanding how the Chechen nationalist struggle was to be linked to Islam later on. That form of Islam was rooted in two Sufi brotherhoods: the Naqshbandiyya and the Qadiriyya. Every Chechen is associated with one of the branches of these brotherhoods, and members of the same clan may belong to different ones. These brotherhoods are also a form of social organization. Nevertheless, they lost a great deal of influence during the Soviet era, when Chechen society took part in the overall movement towards secularization. Chechen Islam, many of whose leaders disappeared, in particular during the deportation in 1944,[6] gave up many of its political aspects at that time and was transformed through an emphasis on Sufi rituals and traditions such as festivals, *zikr*,[7] etc. Respecting those rituals during the deportation played a major role in maintaining Chechen identity.

In addition to the emergence of jihadists[8] in the Russo-Chechen conflict, which we will examine later on, one issue of great importance involves the response to Salafist religious and political ideas, in direct opposition to local Sufism. Two aspects played a crucial role: a generational conflict on the one hand, and a connection to the national struggle on the other.[9]

The generational conflict. Claiming a connection to Wahhabism has enabled young people to challenge clan-based decision-making structures. Through such references young people have succeeded in legitimizing their decision-making capacity. Within the Palestinian context, Islamism has challenged patriarchal authority by referring to a higher source of legitimacy and by establishing a direct reference to the Koran (in essence, playing the Koran off their fathers). Similarly Wahhabism, by challenging Sufism and especially social structures connected to it, has provided an opportunity for young people.[10] It has highlighted a direct connection to God, without any intermediary religious authorities, and built a religious relationship which can take on a more individualistic side in certain contexts, beyond the highly prescriptive rules of that movement and its organization in more or less closed groups. Thus the Wahhabis have often found themselves in direct opposition to village councils. Furthermore, this new religious reference has gone hand-in-hand with the creation of armed groups, which has enabled them to impose their decisions through the use of force. Lastly, in a devastated economy, these groups have provided a great deal of financial assistance.

Social advancement has been possible within these movements through knowledge about Islam. Chechen Sufism has suffered from its failure to transmit such knowledge. Thus, in particular since the institution of Sharia, individuals with expertise on the subject of Islam – acquired over a few years through *ad hoc* training in Arab countries, including a certain familiarity with the language of the Koran – can attain positions upon their return that were previously unthinkable (president of a court, for instance). However, for the time being we lack sufficient information about the sociological profiles of those supporting Wahhabism.

The challenge to the established order has therefore come about through the use of weapons, but also through this reference to knowledge, even if the latter is marked by intense ideology.

The relationship to the national struggle. A new interpretation of the national struggle has also been facilitated by the reference to Islamism. Indeed, during the second Russo-Chechen War some of the Sufi authorities – in particular Kadyrov, a former mufti and combatant – were gradually discredited as the war progressed and repression by the Russians got worse, since they had collaborated with the latter. Although the administration has altered certain attitudes since then, it has continued to apply pro-Russian policies.

On the opposite side, combatant groups such as those led by Basayev have linked Islamism to the national struggle and referred to the figure of the Imam Shamil. The latter, who belonged to the Naqshbandi brotherhood, founded an independent imamate in the 19th century uniting Chechnya and Dagestan, where he established the Sharia. He was defeated and deposed by the Russians in 1859. The rooting of Islam within the national struggle has also been achieved through the notions of *ghazavat* and *jihad*. While *jihad* refers to ''the believer's efforts to improve himself'' (major or inner *jihad*), or to the ''holy war carried out to defend Muslims and their lands'' (minor or outer *jihad*), *ghazavat* specifically designates combat between armies.[11] It was first used in reference to the 19th century Caucasus Wars, and later during the first Russo-Chechen war.

The notion of *jihad* developed here is thus closely tied to references to independence and has only acquired real meaning for certain Chechen combatants within the context of the national struggle. In that sense one may speak of Chechen Islamic nationalism. By referring back to a past involving Islamism and the independence movement, Chechen Islamists are adapting jihadist Islamism to new territory. The creation of an Islamist state could then appear to be an objective which, by reinforcing Chechen society, will also promote its autonomy.

In the same way that the idea of *jihad* developed by Palestinian Islamists suggests not so much a religious agenda as a way of incorporating the national struggle into a religious eschatology – the main objective remaining the territory's independence –, it seems that for the

Chechens this notion should be interpreted more in the context of the past and its glorification. Furthermore, the inclusion of the national struggle within this set of references links this specific form of resistance to other examples of resistance through a criss-crossing chain of identification which has helped Chechnya break out of its isolation, both symbolically and in its attempts to raise funds.

The limited impact of internationalist jihadist groups

For certain – mainly Arab – international jihadist groups, Chechnya is a substitute for Afghanistan. The ideology developed by such groups has turned the Russo-Chechen conflict, like Palestine, into a zone of opposition between oppressed Muslims and infidels. However, they remain very limited in number in relation to the entire Chechen resistance movement; and while their propaganda routinely refers to Chechnya, it is mainly aimed at an Arab Muslim public. The extent of their impact has depended on links to local combatant groups and on territorializing of their references, in other words on how well they adapt to what is at stake locally.

The impact and tactics of armed Wahhabi groups in Chechnya. The first jihadist groups arrived in Chechnya during the first war between 1994 and 1996. Before their arrival, the neo-fundamentalist Wahhabi doctrine had spread in Dagestan under the influence of a Dagestani preacher named Kebedov.[12] Dagestani villages had turned Wahhabi and adopted the Sharia. The term Wahhabi - referring to Wahhabism,[13] a highly conservative form of Sunnism and the official religious doctrine of Saudi Arabia - is often rejected by such individuals themselves, who see it as an oversimplification of their doctrine and too specific a link with Saudi Arabia. The term Salafist is generally used by jihadist groups, although it is not certain that this is widespread in Chechnya. Salafism is an idea that was created in the late 19th century. The term itself comes from *salaf* ("pious ancestor"), and the trend grew out of a desire to return to a purer form of Islam by referring directly to the original texts and by adopting the same lifestyle as the prophet.

This "return" had a political dimension through its resolve to challenge colonialism.[14] Political positions within the Salafist movement are extremely varied, with the jihadist faction merely one of its more extreme forms.[15]

Theories attempting to explain how such doctrines took root usually highlight the usefulness of a form of identification allowing for differentiation from and opposition to the Russians in the post-Soviet context. With respect to Chechnya, there are two different dimensions through which these groups have taken a position in local conflicts and thereby gained an impact – their contribution to the national struggle and their challenging of traditional structures in organizations they were representing.

1. *Integration in the struggle against the Russians.* Indeed these combatants, perceived above all as foreign extremists by the Chechens, were not at all well liked at first. Nevertheless, their alliances with Chechen warlords, the most famous being the one sealed between Basayev and Khattab – a Saudi Arabian Wahhabi and former combatant in Afghanistan – have afforded them a certain measure of integration. This alliance clearly shows their determination to join together with effective groups and to obtain outside financing. As for Khattab, this local "sponsorship" was essential for him because the involvement of his combatants was not well accepted by the population. However, his success against the Russians in the field strengthened the position of his jihadists, and from that time on certain Chechen combatants began making Islamist references. Subsequently, their successes were widely broadcast through videotapes. During the first war, Basayev's most famous military exploit was the February 1995 hostage-taking, following a sortie which aimed to break through the Russian army encircling the Chechens and advance two hundred kilometres to the north of Chechnya. During negotiations the Russian Prime Minister Chernomyrdin announced the end of Russian operations. Although the ceasefire did not hold, it gave the Chechen resistance time to take in the new combatants from the villages destroyed by the Russian

army. That type of operation gave particular visibility to this group of combatants, who nevertheless constituted a minority among the Chechen troops led by Maskhadov. They are estimated to have been three or four thousand in number during this period.

Thus the Wahhabis firmly established themselves through their military successes, and their Islamist discourse was only meaningful in reference to the struggle. For a Chechen combatant, choosing an armed group was more a function of proximity and renown than of ideological orientation. Their relationship to religious practices fluctuated.[16] And the opposition between Sufism and Salafism, which was nevertheless one of the things at stake for foreign combatant groups, held little meaning for the young people who joined such groups and found themselves surrounded by Islamist references linked to the national struggle.

2. *Challenging local authorities?* More or less united with the rest of the Chechen resistance during the first war, these Islamist combatant groups were involved in the extreme division of power in post-war Chechnya. Indeed, their position was threatened within Chechen society. The population favoured negotiating with the Russians and was eager to believe in the accords signed. As the Islamists' presence in the Chechen resistance was disproportionate to their real impact on the population, the end of the war signalled a loss of power for them. The desire to maintain their position manifested itself through two forms of opposition: on the one hand within the independence movement against Maskhadov, who vacillated between compromise and rejection, and on the other hand against the traditional authorities and the Sufi hierarchy. Their position here was not so much a specificity of the Chechen Islamist movements as a standard attitude of warlords eager to maintain their power by carving out fiefdoms - sometimes linked to the criminal world - within which they refused to obey the main authority, in this case Maskhadov. In parallel to that refusal, the Islamists also opposed the local Sufi authorities.

As for the authorities themselves, they struggled against the combatants, challenging the strength they derived from taking part in the war. They sought to keep them out of the villages, to avoid Russian reprisals against civilians. In general they developed an attitude of compromise with the Russians rather than armed struggle, illustrated particularly well by the fate of Kadyrov, the former mufti who ran the pro-Russian Chechen administration from June 2000. In that sense, the authorities constitute a form of opposition to the Islamic nationalists. For the jihadists, there is the added desire to reform Sufi Islam, considered degenerate by comparison with a pure, original Islam. This opposition led to violent internal clashes in July 1998. Within this context, Maskhadov tried in vain to expel the Wahhabis from Chechnya. He obtained no assistance from the Russians.

The Chechen Islamists then proceeded to carry out what could be called both an ideological and a strategic U-turn by strengthening their alliance with the Dagestani Wahhabis. An Islamist congress of Dagestani and Chechen Islamists had been formed in 1997. In 1998 it created an armed division to be led by Basayev. Ideologically speaking, it manifested far greater determination to establish an imamate connected to Shamil. In strategic terms this alliance highlighted a desire for opposition, and clearly led the Islamists to overestimate their influence on the people. Furthermore, the ties between Dagestan and Chechnya prompted them to take into account other aspects at stake such as the conflict between the Wahhabis and the Dagestani government. In August 1999, several hundred combatants commanded by Basayev and Khattab entered Dagestan to "liberate" it and help form an Islamic state united with Chechnya. But the Islamists greatly underestimated the people's opposition to their movement and were faced with local resistance in addition to attacks by the Russian army.

That incident marked the most extreme point in the gap between the Islamists' ideas and the Chechen population. While striving to maintain their position, the Islamists were forced to take things even further. They had a double interest in the situation in Chechnya remaining unstable. First, their influence in the resistance movement – due to their considerable resources – gave them a more important role to play. Secondly, their ideology was only meaningful to people during times of conflict, particularly when conflict intensified and there appeared to be no other way of settling the situation.

Beyond their effective participation in armed groups, what was the Islamists' exact ideological posture?

Which ideological discourse? One cannot talk about one single Islamist discourse in Chechnya, since there are several of them dealing with different issues. Roughly, one could say that references to Islam in Chechnya are threefold: a traditional Sufi Islam which is also involved in the organization of society, an Islamic nationalism, and a jihadist Islamism backed by foreigners. The three discourses are different, as are the leaders of these three trends and their positions on the national struggle. However, these distinctions are not necessarily meaningful to their rank-and-file militants who shift from one to the other. Despite the use of the same vocabulary, a distinct gap is apparent between the discourse developed around Chechnya by the international jihadist movement and that of local Chechen Islamists found on the internet, on videotapes, in declarations made by their leaders, etc. Nonetheless, while one may jump from a territorialized discourse on independence to a de-territorialized discourse with jihadists, the one constant always advanced is the notion of "martyrdom" and the capacity for sacrifice.

For the jihadists, Chechnya has no regional or historical specificity and is merely a place illustrating the oppression of Muslims by *kuffar*. As in Palestine, it has been used *a posteriori* to develop that theory and to legitimize their position by showing the struggle against the abuses of the Russian army in Chechnya. One can distinguish the "non-specialized" jihadist websites, in which Chechnya and Palestine constitute the central – but not the only – themes, from those specifically concerned with Chechnya.

In addition to the websites, Azzam, generally thought to be Al-Qaida's publishing house, has brought out a CD-Rom on Chechnya in Arabic, showing the wartime atrocities and Chechen ambushes against the Russians with a number of personal accounts and wills from *mujahidin*. Videotapes of ambushes led by Basayev and Khattab in Chechnya are also being circulated. This type of media is important because websites are often inaccessible.

In these documents, particularly in the wills of kamikazes and be-queathed videotapes,[17] the Russians are presented as *kuffar*. But the issue of Chechen independence is not the main theme. The videos, photographs and accounts stressing the horror of war, lingering over images of the dead and wounded, and showing the combatants in action are juxtaposed with verses from the Koran. Next to photographs of dead "martyrs" is the text: "Do not think that those killed on the path of Allah are dead. On the contrary, they are living with their God, very well provided for." (Koran III, 169). Similarly, the wills stress the relationship to Allah and *jihad*, with no mention of the Chechen question.

Female martyrdom is featured on the website www.qoqaz.com. Piety and the *shahidat*s' capacity for sacrifice are highlighted: "I know what I'm doing, paradise has its price and I hope it will be the price of paradise. Hawaa Barayev, the sword of *jihad*." A ten-page document explains the specific role women can play within the framework of *jihad*.[18] This glorification of women is always to the detriment of men who have not joined the fight: "A great many women are now taking part in *jihad* and I hope that the men will also participate in *jihad* and not take on the women's role by staying at home.[...] Our ancestors would have killed anyone who tried to touch their wives, but Muslim women are now being attacked and raped in front of those who call themselves men, and they care so little about the honour of their Muslim sisters that they sit there drinking tea while listening to such appalling news."[19]

In contrast to these general invocations, the documents shown on the kavkazcenter website run by the Chechen Udugov – who also has a television channel which he now runs from Qatar –, as well as those on ''martyrdom operations'', are in Russian rather than Arabic; and their discourse is centred around the need to liberate Chechnya. This is the specific framework within which *jihad* is referred to. One example is this declaration made by the hostage-takers at a Moscow theatre,[20] broadcast on Al-Jazeera: ''We have come to the capital to end the war and attain martyrdom here through the path of Allah. We demand an end to the war and the withdrawal of Russian forces.[...] Every nation has a right to self-determination, but Russia has taken that right away from the Chechen people and today we want to take back that right granted us – and to all other nations – by Allah the Most Gracious, the right to freedom and self-determination. The Russian occupants have flooded our country with our children's blood and we have waited a long time for a fair solution [by appealing to] human consciences, but the world is living in a coma and doesn't care about the assassination of innocents.[...] That is why we have chosen this path – the path of jihad for the liberty of the Chechen people.''[21]

There are two opposing discourses. On the one hand, de-territorialized jihadism, and on the other hand, ethnic nationalism evolving towards Islamic nationalism. The two kinds of discourse are not intended for the same audience. Jihadist sites broadcasting mainly in Arabic and English are mainly targeting an Arab-Muslim audience.[22] The same type of competition was found in Palestinian camps in Lebanon, between Islamic nationalism – in movements such as Hamas or Islamic Jihad in this case – and the Salafists' jihadist Islamism. When the mosques were taken over by Islamic nationalist movements such as Hamas, it was perceived as a way of preventing jihadist movements from taking root.[23]

Although somewhat modified by Islamic nationalism, Chechen nationalism's significant influence limits the extent to which jihadist ideology can take root in the country, even if some figures from this movement are present. Islamist ideas are only meaningful for them through an association with the national struggle and its reinterpretation.

An evolving range of actions and the increase in suicide bombings

Is the evolution towards Islamic nationalism a key element in understanding the adoption of a range of actions including suicide bombings? The latter use the *shahid*, or Muslim martyr, as a reference, and in that respect the link might appear quite clear. Suicide bombings are more characteristic of the second war, particularly in 2003. From 2000 to 2003, the Russo-Chechen war was defined on the Russian side by an intensification of methods of massive repression[24] as well as widespread corruption. On the Chechen side, the resistance movement was divided. The people were at the end of their tether. The legitimacy of the pro-Russian administration, already very weak, was not strengthened by the March 2003 referendum, which was widely contested. Furthermore, the combatants clashed over which methods to employ. While ambushes and guerrilla warfare remained the main mode of action, bombings and suicide attacks increased despite Maskhadov's disavowal. Other kinds of operations associated with the idea of martyrdom had been carried out by the Chechens in the past. The main mode of action during the first war therefore consisted of ambushes against the Russian army. However, certain very high-risk attacks designed to help fighters break out of encirclement were presented as suicide attacks. Moreover, some combatants in Islamist battalions celebrated their funerals before going into combat.[25] Nevertheless, it cannot be called suicide in a literal sense except when volunteers were sent over minefields, as in Iran,[26] to allow the main combatants to get out of Grozny under siege. There, they were sure to die. In the two other cases, they used tactics aimed at turning apparently desperate situations around where there was still a chance of survival.[27]

It seems impossible to establish a direct causal link between the increase in suicide bombings and the evolution towards Islamic nationalism, or at least to attribute full responsibility to Islamist organizations in Chechnya. Since the resumption of the conflict, responsibility for the bombings generally was claimed by Basayev until his death in July 2006. But two types of operations must be distinguished. Some, like the taking of hostages at the Moscow theatre, require a great deal of organization, while others – isolated acts with simple targets – seem to be carried out by relatively unorganized individuals.[28] It is unlikely, for example, that Basayev had any real hold over the latter. These acts are carried out by Chechens, and surely not by international jihadist militants. The first suicide attacks using truck bombs were perpetrated in July 2000; but the true intensification and exportation of this mode of action on Russian territory began in December 2002. Nonetheless, the Russian army in Chechnya and the pro-Russian Chechen administration were the targets of the majority of bomb attacks. This specificity highlights the extent to which Chechen society was divided. One of the bombings targeted Kadyrov, the head of the administration.[29]

These diverse elements tend to reinforce the theory of local appropriation of acts such as suicide bombings, which indeed developed through the notion of sacrifice for the cause and the *shahid*, but cannot be considered as the result of indoctrination based on the person's isolation. Moreover, Chechens tend to distance themselves from the jihadist discourse and consider the Islamic nationalists' violence as a form of revenge, the weak man's weapon. The suicide attacks committed by women are associated with the idea of "sacrifice, not in the name of any doctrine, but as an act of revenge or a way of taking justice into one's own hands since one cannot count on the judicial system, nor on help from anyone. Isolation and abandonment by the international community are mentioned constantly."[30]

The history of these women confirms this. People talk of "war widows", and there is always a deceased husband, brother or other relative to justify their desire for revenge. Although these women are increasingly religious, according to Bleuenn Isambard, "the young women who died at the Nord-Ost Theatre in Moscow in October

2002, and others who blew themselves up against Russian targets – or tried to, more or less successfully – were for the most part "modern", educated young women who did not belong to extremist movements. Some were clearly "manipulated" or used as tools, while others decided on their own and made the move alone, or nearly so.[...] Those who were willing to commit such deeds – and even the acts themselves – were appropriated after the fact." The willingness to commit such acts is therefore not the result of indoctrination, but clearly the person's own decision, which is subsequently reinforced and supported, at times by those around him/her, and through religious interpretations stressing the value of sacrifice. The main motivation seems linked on the one hand to a desire to avenge a close relative, and on the other hand to the general context of the situation in Chechnya which is perceived as devoid of hope.

There are some striking analogies here to the case of Palestine, where prospective suicide bombers for the second Intifada (contrary to those in 1994-96), far from being seasoned militants from organizations, were recruited in a much more widespread fashion and often went to the organizations themselves when ready to take action. The same intensification of religious practices took place a few weeks prior to the event. But, contrary to what has occurred in other contexts, the organization did not have to isolate the individuals, who continued to live in their everyday environment up to the last day. As in the case of Chechnya, the suicide bombers in Israel are not recruited from a specific environment, and definitely not from a particularly poor or underprivileged one by the standards of the society as a whole. The Chechen and Palestinian cases are indeed similar, as they both contain broad social breeding-grounds which have been more or less exploited by these organizations, although not created by them. Despair resulting from international indifference must be taken into account as one source for such breeding-grounds.

In parallel with the increase in suicide bombings in Chechnya, the use of religious vocabulary has become more pronounced in talking about the conflict, along with the highlighting of combatants' religious practices – beginning with the "martyrdom" of the suicide bombings. But this does not necessarily reflect any influence from international jihadism. First, one must underline the heritage of past struggles dating back to the 19th century, when Islam was closely tied to anti-colonialism. The use of references from international jihadism indicating Chechnya to be a hotbed of *kuffar* oppression of Muslims is only meaningful if associated with the plan for national liberation in Chechnya. The Islamists' main impact has been through their battalions' exploits, and through a subsequent association – for the time being – with a heroic (but also extremist) image. Conversely, their attempts to change values within Chechen society and their opposition to traditional structures have alienated a segment of the population. However, this may also afford them some credibility with the younger generation, to whom they represent a chance for social advancement and greater power.

Although the reference to martyrdom provides a framework for legitimizing suicide bombings, these mainly grow out of a desire for revenge, of a personal nature in most cases – suicide attacks against the general who killed one's brother, for example –, and as such could potentially find wider support among the Chechen population. That same aspect of revenge – a list of names could be mentioned in a will – is present in Palestinian kamikazes; but injecting the notion of an eschatological *jihad* adds a temporal dimension which allows the lost national struggle to be recast with very long-term prospects for victory. That aspect seems to be missing from the Chechen equation, which perhaps confirms a weaker ideological link between suicide attacks and the Islamic nationalist reinterpretation of the struggle.[31]

5

VIOLENCE AGAINST THE SELF:
THE CASE OF A KURDISH NON-ISLAMIST GROUP

Olivier Grojean

Even if the present-day situation demands a new look at the phenom-enon of martyrdom, it is important to recognize how difficult it is for journalists, observers and researchers alike to give an account of the forms of sacrificial commitment to a political cause. The com-partmentalization of academic disciplines and the methodological problems inherent in this type of study – in particular the "sensitivity" of the subject, but above all the difficulties involved in accessing and processing source materials – are the main reasons for this problem. Nevertheless, a number of researchers have engaged in productive reflection on this type of phenomenon, often favouring a cross-dis-ciplinary approach: temporality, space, violence, sacrifice and the sacred, culture and beliefs are all analyzed in relation to the politi-cal cause being defended. The specificity of "suicide" modes of action however leads most authors to conclude that they should form the subject of a dedicated field of research, as if the object was definitively constructed and defined.

In our view, the main problem derives from the highly polysemous nature of the subject being observed. Beyond etiological or teleologi-cal definitions of the phenomenon of martyrdom, it might be advisable to concentrate on the forms of violence against the self in aid of a political cause. This intentionally broad construction of the subject starts from a hypothesis that has been little explored until now: the relative continuum between "suicidal" modes of action and "suicide" modes of action. This hypothesis in no way suggests that a "suicidal" mode of action (in other words, high-risk action such as a hunger strike) is akin to suicide bombings and other forms of "suicide" commitment (which seem to overturn the very idea of risk); nevertheless the difference in kind generally established between the two would appear to prevent a true understanding of the phenomena of violence against the self.

The aim of this article is therefore to analyze what a hermeneutics of the body can contribute to an understanding of ultimate forms of commitment, starting from the hypothesis that political violence against the self depends on a certain socially constructed relationship in a given context. The example of the Kurds will help us show how a certain *imaginaire* of the body gradually develops which can be mobilized when required by forces that have concretized – or operationalized – certain cultural predispositions. After briefly analyzing the social construction of the body among the Kurds of Turkey and showing how the body can be part of a negotiation process whose objective is to obtain a status, we will then take the example of the Kurdistan Workers Party (PKK) to demonstrate more precisely how commitment is progressively thought of as a means of affirming a truth that abides no alternative. Although not providing a complete explanation, this approach should allow us to pinpoint some possible connections between social identity and ultimate forms of commitment.

Hermeneutics of the body

If violence against the self is considered as an ultimate[1] repertoire of political action available in political arena, a pragmatic definition of the phenomenon begins to emerge, fuelled by at least three motivations. Some forms of ultimate commitment tend initially to flirt with death without always necessarily achieving it (hunger strikes or self-immolation for example): of 164 PKK members or sympathizers who tried to immolate themselves between 9 October 1982 and 2006, less than half of them did in fact die (47%). On the other hand, hunger strikes – which are generally not considered as sacrificial violence – can lead to the death of dozens of militants, as they did during the protest against prison reform in Turkey. We feel that at this stage death should not be considered as a dependent variable in the definition of ultimate forms of commitment.

Furthermore, the protagonists have the option of mixing different types of action. Illegal immigrants sometimes resort to self-mutilation, hunger strikes and self-immolation. Similarly, PKK activists or sympathizers have used hunger strikes, for example – of limited duration or until death[2] –, self-immolations and suicide bombings; the Liberation Tigers of Tamil Eelam (LTTE) resorted to hunger strikes and suicide bombings, and in June 2003 members of the People's Mujahedin Organization of Iran (PMOI) immolated themselves in protest at the arrest of their leader Maryam Rajavi, while others embarked on a hunger and thirst strike. All these examples suggest that it is not appropriate to make a radical distinction between the different phenomena of violence against the self. Certainly suicide bombings, whose purpose is also to destroy the enemy, belong to a register which seems at first to be very different. But we will see that in the case of the Kurds, this technique appears to be strongly linked to the militants' professional ethos. For example, all the suicide bombings by the PKK have been committed by fighters already well trained for war.

Lastly, and crucially we believe, most analyses of self-inflicted violence seem to have one common factor: the body, understood in its political dimension, is often designated as an object able to enlighten the researcher on the phenomena of ultimate commitment. A weapon invented relatively recently, it is in fact also a favourite subject in the study of regimes of subjectivization, in other words, the way in which individuals construct their relationship to the world, think of themselves, organize themselves and act in different contexts. How then does the body become a place, a moment and an object of commitment? How does a person sometimes make the transition from violence against others to a violence whose aim is to destroy both the other and the self? And beyond this, mindful of the fact that the action is sometimes collective and sometimes individual, is it possible to find a link between the protagonists' social identity and the use of violence against the self? Is it appropriate to talk about a certain "culture of the body"[3] within a particular group? The many different trajectories of the protagonists demand caution in this instance.

Furthermore, attempting to introduce the body variable to understand the phenomena of ultimate commitment remains extremely debatable. The main risk lies in the establishment of a monocausal relation between a specific means of action on the one hand and the social characteristics of those who use it on the other, particularly as commitment is always individual, even if the action is undertaken collectively. However, this approach —when conducted with all necessary precaution – has already proved heuristic in the study of hunger strikes (Feldman 1991; Roux 1997; Siméant 1998a). We can thus attempt to make a connection between the "social value" assigned to people and the commitment involved in violence against the self: the weakness of political resources in relation to a dominant adversary, denial of social, legal or political status – of the group and/or the protagonist within this group – are factors which, in addition to a specific socialization dominated by violence, the suffering experienced and sometimes incarceration, seem to lead to a predisposition towards commitment to some forms of violence against the self. In short, certain types of socialization, certain subjectivization regimes (Bozarslan 2004), tend to reduce individuals to their biological bodies, and this might incite some people, in a context that has yet to be determined, to do violence to themselves – even destroy themselves – for a cause.

Violence against the self and the relation to the body: suffering and status

The "Kurdish question" in Turkey, which has been a continual source of conflict and violence since the end of the 19th century, can be enlightening in the study of violence against the self as long as a distinction is made between the social construct of the body among the Kurdish population of Turkey[4] and the ethos constructed within the organizations that have spearheaded Kurdish nationalism since the 1970s. Kurdish nationalism grew faster between 1920 and 1940, as a reaction to Turkish nationalism which was held up as the state ideology after 1923. It gradually became imbued with the social Darwinian elements and racial anthropology that formed the basis of Turkish historiography in the 1930s (Copeaux 1999; Bozarslan 2001). The idea of fighting for the survival of the race or that of the individual as a primordial element of the biological nation then placed the Kurdish body within a complex political system. As a fundamental unit of the nation, the Kurdish body is transcended by its beauty and spirit. But as a participant in the global edifice, it can also be pox-ridden, infecting its limbs, developing as a reaction a theme of unity and the enemy within, as in Turkish historiography. The 1930s also saw the crushing of a number of Kurdish uprisings, often seen as transitions between "primitive rebellions" and "modern" forms of nationalist protest (White 2000). The memory of the various uprisings and their repression, the banning of the Kurdish language, submission to the Turkish educational system, imprisonment and often even torture gradually ravaged these bodies and scarred them indelibly, and the wounds were internalized.

The diseased body then became emblematic of the Kurdish nation. One of the factors that today's observer of the Kurdish social and political scene finds most striking is the insistent attention given to mutilated bodies. For instance, the premises of Kurdish or Turkish associations display portraits of martyrs, and organizations publish a certain number of internal documents (newspapers, reviews) or external literature (leaflets, press releases) filled with photos of tortured bodies and images of destruction. So as to justify their own struggle, the images of bodies of torture victims and the portraits of martyrs associated with the cause being fought are even more eloquent than condemnations of the persecutors. These photographs then can be considered as public acts of condemnation whose purpose is radically to reverse the stigmata of the suffering experienced (Goffman 1975).

The many hunger strikes by militants in Turkey or by Kurdish refugees in Europe can be interpreted in the same way. The hunger strikes are indeed akin to what Schelling called the "power of the weak", in other words, "a related set of tactics that consists of maneuvering one's self into a position in which one no longer has any effective choice over how he shall behave or respond. The purpose of these tactics is to get rid of an embarrassing initiative, making the outcome depend solely on the other party's choice". The common perception of the hunger strike as a type of non-violent action here seems misleading: in escaping the state's hold over his or her own body, the hunger striker is part of a protest against the monopoly of the state's legitimized violence over people's bodies. Furthermore, the hunger striker is crucially challenging the state's monopoly on the attribution of status (Siméant 1998, p. 307). And this last factor seems particularly revealing regarding the status value attributed to the body: the hunger strike is indeed used mainly by people protesting against the legal or political status assigned to them, or for a new status denied them, by the state.

Exclusion from the community of citizens, imprisonment, even humiliation, ill-treatment, rape and/or torture, experienced directly or through the media and "incorporated" into a personal history, are all means of "political objectivization of bodies" (Siméant 1993), emblems of a status of dominated. However, "if like Michel Foucault we regard the question of branding bodies as pertinent, if like Georges Balandier we recognize that the body is a vehicle for political branding, a political operator, then as a corollary we must recognize the possibility of this medium being appropriated by those who have limited access to other forms of protest" (Siméant 1998, p. 309). This is particularly the case with illegal migrants,[5] but also of all the nationalist militants demanding the status of a recognized minority or a legitimate political organization, or political prisoner status. This strategic recourse to violence against the self could imply that it is no more than a rational instrumentalization of a person's own culture, of their own stigmata.[6] But the many other forms of more spontaneous violence against the self – attempts at self-immolation by illegal immigrants, or banging one's heads violently against the walls or windows of a bus, as some Kurdish refugees from Iraq did at the French refugee camps of Sangatte – show the extent to which the *imaginaire* of the afflicted body can be mobilized subconsciously and without premeditation during action.

Ultimate forms of commitment: purity and truth

The body, symbolizing the status of being dominated, can also become the sole means for a person to demonstrate their loyal devotion to the leader and to endorse the truth of the cause. More precisely, as Bozarslan points out, in the cases of nihilism and self-sacrifice the individuals might seek to preserve the purity of their own engagement, body and mind, by using violence. In both cases the subject, in the sociological sense of the word, is unable to become a positive subject. He or she cannot envisage the realization of his or her aims in a constructive process that would necessarily involve some degree of compromise. The destruction of his or herself thus becomes the very condition of his or her emergence as a subject." (Bozarslan, 2004) This theory helps us to understand how the PKK embarked on a path of radical reversal of the suffering experienced, by reinterpreting Kurdish national history and historiography from the point of view of a present situation marked by violence.

Founded in 1978, the PKK was built on the *imaginaire* of the ravaged body in interaction with its regional environment, which was scarred by the defeat of Barzani's movement in Iraq in 1975, the Iranian revolution and the 1980 coup d'état in Turkey. First and foremost a nationalist organization, it espoused Marxism-Leninism, like many other organizations, enabling it to make particularist demands while belonging to a universalist *imaginaire*. The charismatic leadership of Abdullah Öcalan and the meta-ideology of the movement thus became major vectors of subjectivization which demanded the birth of a new Kurdish man, in the leader's image. This new man is a model soldier, extremely well disciplined, obedient to his superiors, who must willingly accept any job and any hardship, even going as far as self-sacrifice. The first hunger strikes and suicides of the founding militants in Diyarbakır prison in 1982 contributed to the development of a martyr cult, which then extended to all the fighters. But in the party's iconography, the bodies of these martyrs are never wounded, mutilated or burned: only the face of the "future" martyr appears.[7] The fighters can also be depicted either in fatigues or in civilian clothing, sometimes armed with a Kalashnikov, flanking Abdullah Öcalan. The image of the disciplined, smiling body, on which the stigmata of the violence suffered do not yet appear but are already inscribed and have only to reveal themselves in death, are symbols of devotion to the cause and to the leader.

The notions of purity and innocence and, conversely, of impurity and guilt then become central to the PKK militants' sense of commitment. There is a striking parallel between the purity of the blood spilled and the purity of the cause on the one hand, and the impurity of the living body and the impurity of the social universe to which the protagonist belongs on the other. However, if we exclude suicide acts in prison, most of the PKK's forms of sacrificial action have taken place when the party's strategy suffers defeat: 6 attempts at self-immolation in Switzerland and Germany just one month after the end of the first unilateral cease-fire on the part of the PKK; 12 self-immolations in several German cities in 1994, a few months after the ban of the PKK in Germany; 3 suicide bombings in Turkey and 7 self-immolations between June and October 1996, a few months after the failure of the second unilateral ceasefire; a wave of 85 self-immolations and 12 suicide bombings after the PKK's third ceasefire and then Öcalan's arrest and apologies in 1998-99. It is as if the leadership's attempts at negotiation and their failure had pushed some militants – or some tendencies of the movement expressing the wishes of the rank and file – to radicalize the conflict anew, to avoid all "compromise".

The examples of a few PKK women martyrs can be particularly instructive. It does indeed seem to be a feeling of defiance vis-à-vis superiors of their own group that distinguishes most of their sacrificial forms of action. Within "traditional" Kurdish society, the men's place of honour, but more generally that of the family and the nation, is primarily focused on the woman's body (*namûs*). Woman is always a potential traitress, and men are supposed to be suspicious of her and seek to control her body and her sexuality. A woman who dishonours her husband or her family (hymen already broken before marriage, adultery) must be killed, or preferably commit suicide in order to restore the honour of the group. Entry into the PKK, which advocates women's "emancipation", often puts the young woman militant in conflict with her family milieu, despite mechanisms to facilitate this transition (the organization becomes the guarantor of the *namûs*, for example). But in the PKK historiography, a combination of tradiional and new elements, the forms of emancipation are of two types: the woman-mother, whose job is to transmit a sense of Kurdish ethnicity to the children, and the woman-at-arms, disciplined and obedient to the image of the Kurdish "new man".

The internalization of these models then encourages any young militant woman – who is not permitted to marry – to become a fighter. But sometimes the party refuses to send women into the mountains, because they are either too young or not fit to fight, or because their families categorically oppose their going. It would seem that the self-immolations of Ronahî and Berivan in Mannheim in 1994 were a response to being prevented from taking part in military struggle. The image of the woman-martyr having been created[9] and examined theoretically in 1992 by Öcalan in his book *Kadın ve Aile Sorunu* ("The question of women and the family"), and some female political militants having experienced this form of commitment, female PKK guerrilla fighters could now take part in suicide bombings "for love of humanity and of life".[10] This however does not indicate a definitive switch from one mode of action to another: suicide bombings and self-immolations continued to exist side by side as part of the movement's repertoire until Öcalan was sentenced to death in June 1999, a sentence converted to life in prison. In February 1999 the attempted self-immolation of a female party member in Denmark also seems to have been inspired both by respect for Öcalan and by a sense of defiance vis-à-vis certain party hierarchs: anguish at possible internal betrayal against Öcalan and at the likelihood that the party would not allow her to go into the mountains where she had been asking to be sent for several years. In this instance, self-immolation belonged to the *imaginaire* of armed struggle and guerrilla warfare: as she was unable to construct a positive social identity, death in martyrdom in Europe was the only alternative, enabling her to show the "true" path to liberation and emancipation.

Social identities, mode of action and political commitment

The development and widespread dissemination of an *imaginaire* of the afflicted body do not alone explain a person's decision to take action. Not all Kurds resort to self-inflicted forms of violence, and not all members of the PKK have the intention of dying for the cause. Perhaps an analysis of the different forms of commitment within a movement would allow us better to explain the correlation between the relationship to the body and the mode of action used. It does indeed appear that ultimate forms of commitment emerge when the demands of the protagonists became inextricably bound up with their social identity.[11]

All forms of violence against the self first raise the question of the risks involved: risk of death, risk of the protagonist or the organization becoming outlawed, as well as the risk that the militant will simply not be able to rise to the commitment required. The question of risk is then closely related to whether the decision to go into action is taken individually or collectively.[12] What is very specific about the hunger strike is that the striker takes his or her own body hostage (Roux 1997), and associates himself or herself with a negotiation process that makes the other party responsible for the associated risk of death. Everything depends on the threat and the likelihood of "going through with it to the end", and the risk is then translated onto the opponent. But the organization of a hunger strike of illegal immigrants and of a "political" hunger strike in Europe for the Kurds of the Middle East is very different. Whereas in the first instance the protagonist implicates his or her own body (individual action constructed relatively often on a collective mode) and links their fate to a reply from the authorities, it is very much a matter of numbers rather than duration that is the hallmark of the PKK hunger strikes in Europe (the action is then collective in that it is endorsed by a previously constructed collective).[13] In this case, the risk is lower and is often akin to an action of support for the Kurds of Turkey who may be engaged in a "death fast" in Turkish prisons.[14] Nevertheless, the strike remains a means of demonstrating the genuineness of a person's commitment and the transformation of their personality with a view to becoming a "true Kurd" both to the world and to the leader.

But as soon as there is truly (to avoid saying "statistically") a risk of death, a different logic comes into play which is more akin to that of a suppression of the risk (Bozarslan 2004). The author of a suicide bombing – individual or collective, as in the attacks of 11 September, 2001 – programmes his own death and completely puts aside the question of risk. The Kurdish prisoner who embarks on an unlimited collective hunger strike in the Turkish prisons also knows that he has no chance of survival if he sees his action through to the end. In all these cases, when the action is decided by the organization that claims responsibility for it, it is most often at the suggestion of the protagonist who declares himself ready to carry out the suicide operation or death fast. It is important to distinguish the individual nature of the commitment from the collective responsibility linked to that commitment, in other words, to explore the social construction of the wish to die for the cause as part of a group. When the demands are considered to be unjustified in the eyes of the world and sometimes hig-ranking members of their own group, they are discarded in favour of an action that will be more effective in proving quite simply that the cause is "true" and fits into the scheme of absolute necessity.

The action of the young female PKK militant who pours petrol over herself before setting herself alight in the streets of London, doubtless believing she will not survive, seems to be more a reversal of the risk. The socialization of the young female PKK recruits, who can only see the world through the prism of the cause and the party and can only project themselves into a pure, "true" ideal, tends to produce extremely precarious psychological situations as soon as doubt arises. If their social identity is absolutely and completely bound up with Abdullah Öcalan and the cause, the young male or female militant is all the more afraid of survival than of death when all his or her points of reference collapse. If he or she has internalized the leader's discourse on personal responsibility and perfection – always sought-after but unattainable – then only death makes them capable of the commitment required and the love owed to the leader. Here, it is indeed the fear of not being capable of making a strong enough commitment that seems to motivate the action.[15]

Lastly, violence against the self raises the question of who the audience and the target are. Johanna Siméant (1998) points out in relation to the hunger strikes in France that the effectiveness of violence against the self necessarily lies in the emotion that can be stirred in those who witness the body's suffering. Thus the hunger strike (which differs from the death fast) appeals to public opinion while bearing testimony to the strikers' determination to reach a negotiated solution with the opposition: here, temporality is central. But once again, it is very different when the protagonist is involved in an action of non-negotiation, which is irreversible and strictly one-off. It naturally appeals to the community of citizens and international public opinion, but the purpose of the act seems to be much more to affirm his or her "true" identity within the group. Through a process of creating heroes, self-immolations thus sometimes seem to be aimed at strengthening the unity of the committed group and preventing defections, for example the occupation of a motorway in Germany or a hunger strike in France.

Suicide bombing, which by definition seeks rather to kill the enemy than to "make him feel guilty", is also said to be often a means of restoring the balance of deaths while at the same time creating "exemplary" heroes likely to unify the nation again. But how is it possible to understand that the suicide bomber is seeking to kill everyone else and blow himself up at the same time? At this point it is fitting to reintroduce the question of the professionalization of those involved. All the suicide bombings organized by the PKK are in fact the work of seasoned fighters, already conversant with guerrilla techniques and prepared to kill for the cause. Two-thirds of the PKK's 17 suicide bombings, incidentally, were carried out by women who were all guerrilla fighters. From 1995, the question of whether the operations were effective became central to the party: the failure of the military strategy, which could not be blamed on Öcalan, affected the fighters who lapsed through lack of faith or commitment. Groups of "fedayeen" were trained in deadly operations which were thought to be more effective and designed to convince the enemy of the guerrilla fighters' determination. According to government sources, the second unilateral PKK ceasefire, which remained without a response from the Turkish government for more than six months, should have been broken by a suicide attack on 10 June 1996, but was prevented by the Turkish security forces. Less than three weeks after, on 30 June 1996, the first suicide attack was launched in Tunceli. While bombings against civilians took place as far back as 1993, the main targets of the subsequent suicide bombings were always military or state targets.[16] Öcalan's custody in Italy in 1998, his arrest in Kenya and his extradition to Turkey in 1999 no doubt incited some groups of militants to attack the population; responsibility for the attacks on civilians is often claimed by Apo's Falcons of Revenge (Apo is Öcalan's *nom de guerre*). However, suicide attacks seem to have been strictly confined to a desire for self-destruction while at the same time attempting to kill the enemy when the militant's professional ethos permitted it. But this military strategy has obviously failed as well: besides the dead militants, fewer than 30 people actually died in these 17 attacks, and this fact again underlines the value of self-sacrifice in the PKK *imaginaire*.

The study of the social construction of the relationship to the body thus seems to offer a fertile territory for investigating ultimate forms of commitment. Paying attention to the context of action can indeed enable us to identify connections between the protagonists' social identities and different forms of commitment while refraining from making an automatic link between the social characteristics of the individuals and their chosen modes of action. These comments pertaining to the Kurds do not in any way claim to be universally valid: the eschatological-type violence of the Palestinian or Chechen "martyrs", which is sometimes aimed at the civilian population rather than military targets, tends to demonstrate that the idea of revenge could be symptomatic of a new relation to authority and to the principle of justice which this authority is supposed to guarantee. But in each of these cases, as in that of the Kurds, it seems possible to navigate between types of action whose object is to demand a status and other forms of commitment permitting the affirmation of an alternative truth, following the medium-term evolution of a certain relationship to the body.

Beyond that, suicide action often appears as a means of challenging both elements of the leadership in a person's own camp and the supremacy of the enemy while at the same time invoking the original principles of the cause. When public opinion closes its eyes, when the upper echelons of the hierarchy end up advocating negotiations with the enemy, thus violating the fundamental principles of the original cause – while suffering still abounds – and ends up even refusing its members' trust, a new hero needs to come forward: not an impartial arbiter, but an all-powerful authority who will impose a truth on all and against all. Although the demand for status can thus appear to be a dialogic construct aiming at compromise, the affirmation of a truth seems to be part of a rationale that refutes bygone unanimity and the failure of the cause, denies reality any sort of legitimacy and constructs its own system of dichotomous values.

BIBLIOGRAPHY

Bozarslan, Hamit (2001). "Quelques remarques sur le discours historio-graphique kurde en Turquie: 1919-1980", *Asien Afrika Lateinamerika*, vol. 49, pp. 47-71.

Bozarslan, Hamit (2004). *Violence in the Middle East: From Political Struggle to Self-sacrifice*, Princeton, Markus Wiener Publishers.

Copeaux, Etienne (1997). *Espace et temps de la nation turque*, Paris, CNRS Editions.

Feldman, Allen (1991). *Formation of Violence: the Narrative of the Body and Political Terror in Northern Ireland*, University of Chicago Press.

Fliche, Benoît (2000). "Quand cela tient à un cheveu. Pilosité et identité chez les Turcs de Strasbourg", *Terrain*, n° 35, September 2000, pp. 155-65.

Foucault, Michel (1963). *Naissance de la clinique*, Paris, PUF.

Goffman, Erving (1986). *Stigma: Notes on the Management of Spoiled Identity*, New York, Touchstone.

Harding, Timothy and Romano La Harpe (1998). "L'autopsie: violence or réparation?", in Michel Porret (ed.), *Le corps violenté, du geste à la parole*, Geneva, Droz, pp. 287-92.

Larzillière, Pénélope (2001). "Le "martyre" des jeunes Palestiniens pendant l'Intifada Al-Aqsa: analyse et comparaison", *Politique Etrangère*, n° 66, pp. 937-51.

Memmi, Dominique (1998). "Introduction: la dimension corporelle de l'activité sociale", *Sociétés Contemporaines*, n° 31, pp. 5-13.

Roux, Jacques (1997). "Mettre son corps en cause: la grève de la faim, une forme d'engagement public", in Jacques Ion (ed.), *Engagement public et exposition de la personne*, Paris, Éditions de l'Aube, p. 111-34.

Schelling, Thomas (1960). *The Strategy of Conflict,* London, Oxford University Press.

Siméant, Johanna (1993), "La violence d'un répertoire. Les sans-papiers en grève de la faim", *Cultures et Conflits*, n° 9-10.

Siméant, Johanna (1998). *La cause des sans-papiers*, Paris, Presses de Sciences Po.

6

THE DISTINCTIVE DEVELOPMENT OF ISLAMIST VIOLENCE IN ALGERIA

Luis Martinez

The image of the deterritorialized "terrorist martyr" belonging to a transnational network emerged after the attacks of September 11, 2001.[1] The fear inspired by this new figure in the international community is embodied in a "war on terrorism", but ultimately it obscures the reasons for the appearance of this phenomenon.

An analysis of the violence in Algeria during the last decade shows that the involvement of Algerians in international networks is a result of the eradication of their national organizations. In short, the violence has become de-localized, and so has the choice of targets. Seen from this angle, the suicide bombings perpetrated against "the Western world" are part of a different process from such bombing by guerrillas fighting against regimes they consider to be infidel and illegitimate. These attacks are designed to punish, exert pressure, or provoke a state of war between the West and Islam, so as to give external credibility to a violence previously confined within the Muslim states. The terrorist's sacrifice only gives him martyr status if he attacks '"the infidel"; he has to see the Muslim society in which he lives as apostate so as to justify his violence, or emigrate so as to attack a more or less imaginary West inhabited by non-believers.

In Algeria, commitment to armed Islamism did not begin with the concept of sacrifice or martyrdom, for the repertoires of actions on which these combatants drew were deeply rooted in the local "war culture".[2] Violence is not an instrument of sacrifice, but of change. The use of violence brings about social transformation and the accumulation of wealth, as has been demonstrated in the study of the "emirs" (chiefs of the armed groups).[3] A "sectarian" approach to society gradually emerged, especially among the GIA (Groupe Islamique Armé / Armed Islamic Group), facilitating the transition to mass violence against a society deemed to be ungodly. This violence against Muslim civilians has "tainted" the Algerian Islamists and undermined the validity of their *jihad* in the eyes of the people. For young Algerians enlisting in international Islamist networks warring against "the Crusaders and the Jews", does this represent a means of redemption through self-sacrifice in the form of suicide bombing?

Violence against the state, not against the self

The volunteer is able make the transition to a suicide bombing strategy because he believes he is a "pure" being in a sullied world. However, the Algerian Islamist fighters have always defined themselves not as "pure" but as "righteous" beings: the purpose of their actions is to bring about change here on earth. Renunciation of the world as represented by suicide bombing does not apply to them, because to them, "justice" can be achieved by fighting against the state, the embodiment of the Taghout.[4] The state will be defeated, very classically, by an urban and rural guerrilla war supported by the population, and a just Islamic state will be founded on the principles of Sharia.

Until the large-scale massacres of civilians (1997–98), the Algerian Islamist groups were convinced that "the people" were on their side and that the regime was nothing but a Mafia system protected by the national army. The "enemies of Islam", perceived as outsiders, would be killed. It was only after 1996 that certain groups, disappointed that "the people" were not sufficiently behind "the cause" and were even taking up arms to defend themselves, stepped up the killing of civilians. This did not take the form of suicide bombings, but of massacres.[5] Unlike the Palestinian suicide bombers who seek to enter paradise through their martyrdom, these Islamists created hell on earth for all those who opposed their determination to establish an Islamic state, for whatever reason. In their view, Algeria had been surreptitiously transformed into a land of *jihad* where the state was the Devil, where the national army was likened to the French colonial army, and where society was divided into believers and traitors – the latter coming under the heading of "Jews and Crusaders". This metamorphosis of Algeria into a land of infidels prepared the GIA fighters mentally and psychologically to see Algerians who resisted them as "enemies of Islam" who had to be destroyed.

The violence of the GIA: Algeria as a land of infidels. "Do seek family consent! But if you do not receive it, continue regardless, the *jihad fi sabil lilah* is greater than blood ties": this principle of commitment to the armed Islamist groups made it clear that family ties no longer acted as a curb on violence.[6] During the bloodiest years of the decade (1993–98), the GIA fighters took on the attributes of a new family thanks to sacrificial rites.[7] In addition to "local murders"[8] there were the massacres of villagers that confirmed the fighters' enduring commitment. It is true that these killings were rewarded by booty – young women, money and material goods – which the GIA emirs considered part of Islamic tradition. The Mufti of Marseilles remarked that "the men of the GIA act in a very canonical manner, which is why they can equally be seen praying or raping.[...] Women are part of the spoils of war according to this same canonical reasoning.[...] I condemn the hypocrisy of the Muslim theologians who speak out against these practices and the massacres, it is true, but do not question the theology that underpins them. They must seize this opportunity to challenge the sanctity of Muslim law, especially certain points that provide these barbarians with a pretext."[9]

The violence of the GIA met with incomprehension on the part of Muslims and censure from the leaders of international Islamist organizations. Far from being part of "Islamic orthodoxy", the GIA appears as a deviant tendency and above all a specifically Algerian phenomenon. How is possible to make sense of this extreme violence? Analyses of political Islam to date have pinpointed two strategies: a "bottom-up Islam" in the hands of grassroots associations working to Islamize society; and a "top-down Islam" seeking to change the state by attacking its regime. In the case of Algeria, the GIA's violence is protean, aiming to be total, because the state, its political regime and society are "enemies of Islam". But in fact it belongs to a political imagination where there is very little room for Islam from the perspective of the historical structures that are the legacy of the War of Independence (1954–62) and the colonial war of occupation (starting in 1830).[10] These two periods effectively constitute founding myths. Whereas the War of Independence led to the "rebirth of the Algerian state", the colonial war broke down the organization of society and humiliated the population. This society was only able to regain its dignity through the "martyrdom" of one and a half million *shahideen* (witnesses or martyrs).

In other contexts, the aim of suicide bombings is often to force politicians to enter into negotiations. However, the GIA emirs seek not to negotiate compromises between the protagonists, but rather to destroy the opponent in the tradition of all-out war. Suicide bombings would therefore be ineffective. The motto of the GIA, attributed to Qari Saïd,[11] one of its ideologists, is: "No dialogue, no truce, no reconciliation". Which prompted H'Mida Layachi to say that the GIA emirs are "hardliners who have already proved this to be so by attacking those who have negotiated with the government – traitors in their eyes. They would probably even refuse a general amnesty if one were offered to them."[12]

In fact, GIA violence belongs to a bygone era and is aimed at establishing a new order that is religious rather than political.[13] For the GIA, the purpose of action is no longer to change the balance of political power or overthrow the regime, but to overturn the social order.[14] This particular relationship to violence generally meets with incomprehension and revulsion, but sometimes also with admiration: then the GIA fighters appear as "real Muslims" who are "rising up" to sacrifice themselves in the name of Islam. It remains to be understood how they interpret their religion. Although nowadays Arab-Muslim societies are free from the colonial yoke, in their eyes the Islamic religion continues to be persecuted. And so they feel duty-bound to save it, even re-establish it. Their objectives are thus not political, and the project of an Islamic state on their agenda is only a utopia needed to maintain the pressure and combative energy required for liberation. In this sectarian vision, the GIA feels it is on a mission to save an endangered Islam. The emergence of such radical trends is not new. The big difference is the use of cruelty as an instrument.

Through what political, social and psychological mechanism did the GIA fighters come to believe that the Islamic religion was under threat in Algeria? What do they imagine? Even though, as numerous observers have pointed out, recruitment to the GIA has dried up, these groups are still operational after more than a decade of activity. How can the persistence of this violence be explained? Elsewhere, armed Islamist organizations' repertoires of action are based on the principles of resistance, as in the case of Hezbollah in Lebanon, or of self-defence, as with the armed Palestinian organizations, or independence, as in Chechnya. But with the GIA, violence is associated with ideological purification. Apart from the view that "the Jews and the Crusaders" must be eliminated, its purpose is also to "clean up" the social order. Despite the obstacles, its aim is to create favourable conditions for a social and political order that fulfils the requirements of a reinvented Islamic state. The violence of the Islamist organizations is stoked by the memory of the victory of the nationalists who, despite the crushing balance of power in favour of the colonial power, managed to establish an independent state. This heroic resistance of the

Algerians, "from the emir Abdelkader to the FLN (Front de Libération National/National Liberation Front)", constitutes the unwaver-
ing basis of the belief in change through violence.

The AIS or the attempt to impose order on the violence. Confronted with
these excesses, the AIS (Armée Islamique du Salut/Islamic Salvation
Army), founded in 1994, sought to impose order. The chaos provoked
by the GIA was very soon perceived by the AIS emirs as extremely
dangerous. They began by claiming that the GIA had been infiltrated
by the state security service in an attempt to sow discord and bring
about a turnaround of the population in favour of the regime. Then
they gradually recognized that in most cases it was a matter of a genuine choice, but one founded on a "deviant" ideology. The violence of
the GIA was so excessive and counter-productive that it was bound to
be misunderstood. The AIS's attitude to war was not that of the GIA.
Whereas the AIS sought to use arms to create a climate conducive to
negotiations with the army, the violence of the GIA was independent
of any political agenda. The AIS was overwhelmed by the GIA's strategy of all-out war. Aspiring initially to build an Islamic army on the
model of a national army, disciplined and respecting a certain code of
war, the AIS found itself powerless against the groups that attacked
society rather than the security forces. Thus in difficulties on the military front, it also feared that the two fighting organizations would
be confused, and so constantly condemned acts that went against its
ethos: "The apostate regime blames certain abominable operations attacking the defenceless people on the *jihad*.[...] In response to these
falsehoods, the AIS replies that it is innocent of all these acts and that
it has never given the order to attack a woman, burn down a school
or hospital or to carry out any other operation that goes against our
religion'.[15]

In fact, the AIS dreamed of arousing a nationalist fervour in the
population similar to that created by the FLN in its heyday, but which
had abated as a result of economic failure, poverty and corruption.
As opposed to the GIA, it tended to hold the people sacred and tried

to appear as the only legitimate new player.[16] In short, if the GIA was re-enacting the scorched earth policy of the OAS (Organization Armée Secrete/Secret Army Organization), the AIS had the utopian ambition of rebuilding a popular army on the model of the ALN (Armée de Libération Nationale/National Liberation Army). There was an ongoing concern to set up and develop a structure for the armed organization, despite the difficulties encountered. The emirs of the AIS clearly belonged to the same tradition as the *mudjahidin* of the War of Independence (1954–62), albeit without measuring the contradictions inherent in their actions. The slogan "You have liberated the land, we will liberate the minds" presented the AIS fighters with some formidable challenges: how was it possible to "liberate" minds without doing violence to society? The deliberate confusion between the War of Independence, waged to create an independent state, and the war to liberate minds, waged to establish an Islamic state, could only lead to civil war.

In effect, the construction of the enemy in the minds of the AIS Islamists was based on equating the regime with the colonial system. It ignored the fact that apart from the generals and bureaucrats who were accused of lining their pockets from the state's coffers, the FLN-state had deep roots within the country and continued to represent a large proportion of society as best it could. The AIS had no choice but either to attack society physically or to lay down its arms. And yet, in its view: "*Jihad* is not a suicide, a way out for those who are in a rut, such people are contemptible; nor is it a form of vengeance for those who want to settle old scores, such people are full of hatred; nor is it an uncertain enterprise for adventurers and the exiled; nor an anarchist movement with no criteria or rules that recruits runaways and desperados; nor a blind point of honour as practised by the ignorant; nor a blind rush forward, which would indicate a lack of vision or any programme."[17] But the explosion of violence became widespread; the regime responded to the violence of the GIA with "all-out war".[18]

On 21 September 1997, Madani Mezrag, emir of the AIS, released a communiqué in which he "ordered all the company commanders to end combat operations from 1st October and appealed to the other groups fighting for religious interests and those of the nation to rally to this call". He had a dual objective: to obtain negotiations with the army and to dissociate himself from the policy of civilian massacres perpetrated by the GIA.

The AIS failed to channel the "desire for dissidence" of the Islamists anxious to do battle with the regime. The GIA would exhaust itself in this extreme violence. And in 1998, a group of fighters broke away and set up a new armed organization, the Groupe Salafiste pour la Prédication et le Combat (GSPC)/the Salafist Group for Preaching and Combat.

The GSPC: looking to the wider world for a breath of fresh air. The GIA policy of civilian massacres was being challenged from within the Islamist guerrilla movement, and this led to splits. Not only did the GIA alienate society, but its violence drew censure from international Islamist organizations. September 1998 saw the birth of a new armed organization which condemned the direction taken by Zitouni, the emir of the GIA. Internally, the Islamist guerrilla war seemed to have embarked on a process of self-destruction that was gradually cutting it off from society. In short, the GIA was on its way to destroying the foundations laid down by the FIS during its legitimate period (1989–91), thus bearing out Michel Wieviorka's inversion theory of terrorist groups.[19] It seemed vital for the Islamist fighters to open up internationally. On the military front, the emirs sought networks that would help consolidate their armed groups which were struggling at home. But it was above all at the ideological level that there seemed to be total confusion. The ideologists of the guerrilla war had led the troops into an impasse. Indeed, the attempts to overthrow the Taghout and terrorize the "people" had unforeseen effects. The fear of a collapse of the Algerian state led to international support for the regime, and the policy of massacres resulted in the arming of civilians. In short, the state and society's capacity to resist had been underestimated.

Hassan Hattab's Salafist Group for Preaching and Combat found a new fighting ideology in the World Islamic Front for Jihad Against Jews and Crusaders established by Osama Bin Laden, which gave its guerrillas the second wind they needed to sustain the war against the regime. Initially, the GSPC set about reorganizing the armed groups that were still active. It advocated a new definition of the enemy, now confined solely to the security services, and condemned violence against civilians.[20] Between 1998 and 2001, the GSPC maintained a level of heavy violence but there was no comparison with the combined brutality of the AIS and the GIA perpetrated between 1993 and 1997. President Bouteflika's "civil harmony" policy, introduced in 1999, brought around six thousand Islamist fighters back into society. The hope of a genuine reconciliation created a general mood of optimism and gave rise to the hope that the era of violence was finally over. The revival of the armed Islamist groups no longer seemed assured, even though disaffected youth offered a fertile breeding ground. But it was above all at the ideological level that the Islamist guerrilla war had lost its appeal. It was therefore the need to restore the credibility of the armed groups that made the GSPC enter the international arena.

It is from this perspective that the alleged relations between this group and Al-Qaida should be analyzed, for the links between the Algerian Islamist groups and international networks seem to go back a long way. As early as 1992, the "first links between the GIA and the Bin Laden network" could be observed, according to Labévière. Throughout that decade, and particularly after 1998 with the growing power of the GSPC, the regime had exploited these relations in order to stress that the Islamist groups were foreign to Algerian society; but, as elsewhere, the attacks of September 11 marked an abrupt turning point, in that the war on terror declared by the Bush administration made this type of interpretation more acceptable. To establish the existence of close, regular ties between the Islamist groups and Al-

Qaida, the government resorted to oversimplifications.[21] Labévière remarks: "I do not believe for one moment in Al-Qaida's capacity to organize internationally, in particular to set up a branch called the GSPC in Algeria. I believe that the GSPC needs Bin Laden's network to legitimize its murderous violence, rather than the other way round."[22] In fact, the Al-Qaida label was sufficiently attractive and respected to enable the GSPC to regain endorsement for the Islamist guerrilla war. The perception of the GSPC as a cog in the Al-Qaida organization given a specific task seems to be pure fantasy, as is the official statement that "the role of the GSPC in Al-Qaida's strategy goes beyond the Algerian frontiers".[23] And yet, in 2002, the idea of a national harmony measure to assist the GSPC divided the armed groups. But the addition of the GSPC to the US State Department's list of terrorist organizations finally made it possible to envisage the reintegration of its fighters into society.[24]

The collapse of the Taliban regime in Afghanistan led to an international redeployment of the "Arabs" who were settled there. According to the Algerian authorities, the mission of the supposed Al-Qaida representative for the Maghreb and Saharan Africa, Emad Abdelouahid Ahmed Alouane (alias Abu Mohamed, a Yemeni), killed on 12 September 2002 in Algeria, was to assess the situation in Algeria so as to help the fighters from Egypt and North Africa in Afghanistan to settle there. And yet the GSPC had stated, in a communiqué dated 21 September 2001, that its objective was "*jihad* against the Algerian regime" only.

It is true that the determination to attack the West, and France in particular, has long existed among the armed Islamist groups in Algeria. There have been numerous attacks, from the hijacking of an Airbus in 1994 by a GIA commando planning to blow up the Eiffel Tower to the Paris bombings of 1995 and 1996. The feeling that France's unconditional support for the Algerian regime was responsible for the defeat of the guerrilla campaign partially explains this desire to export the conflict. It was also a question of demonstrating that despite the army's triumphant communiqués, the Islamist groups still had the capacity to strike the Algerian regime's main ally, France.

Furthermore, in 1994–95 Quebec opened its doors to the North African countries; after drawing its French-speaking immigrants from the war-torn former French territories (Vietnam, then Lebanon), the province became interested in the Algerian Francophone population, one of the largest in Africa, as a source of new immigrants. The Islamists took advantage of this opportunity, using legal and illegal channels to emigrate there to set up organized cells. This was of some concern to the French and European authorities, as after three years these thousands of Algerian students, Canadian passports in hand, would be free to enter Europe without a visa. In 1999 the first Algerian Islamists suspected of planning attacks in Canada and the USA were arrested.[25] That said, the GSPC still adhered to its initial objective: the overthrow of the Algerian regime. The redefinition of the enemy, the reorganization of the armed groups and the taking over of the overseas networks were the political, military and financial instruments necessary for the – utopian – fulfilment of this goal.

The quest for salvation, or how to close the lid on Pandora's box

The war on terror launched by the president of the USA endorsed the Algerian political and military leaders' analytical perspective. During an international colloquium on terrorism held in Algiers in October 2002, Redha Malek, former prime minister and member of the member of the High Council of State, declared: "Fundamentalist terrorism draws inspiration from the Afghanistan war; it was spread with the help of the Gulf oil monarchies and the CIA, implemented by the former FIS (Front Islamique du Salut/Islamic Salvation Front) and encouraged by the laxism of the authorities at the time. The rise of the FIS, in 1991 and 1992, coincided with the return of the Afghan Algerians (2,000 to 3,000 men) who spearheaded the terrorist violence." This destabilization of Algeria by Afghanistan was also highlighted by General Belkheir who confirmed during an interview: "I have no regrets. I made the choice of sparing Algeria the fate of Afghanistan. There was a heavy price to pay, but it avoided the worst: an outright civil war with millions of victims and refugees."[26]

The Islamist armed groups after September 11: a rereading of the violence. The armed Islamist groups are often perceived schematically as part of a conspiracy fomented by Al-Qaida. The internal developments and socio-political processes that led to the emergence of these Islamist movements are ignored in favour of sweeping generalizations. Furthermore, the attacks of September 11 reignited the perception of an "Islamic" religion that was dangerous and produced violent and murderous excesses. Until now, this perception was based on Shiite Islam and the martyrdom of the Bassidji in Iran or the Hezbollah in Lebanon was seen as a caricatural illustration of it.[27] In the wake of the attacks in New York and Washington, the political determination to extend this image to all the armed Islamist organizations in the world resulted in the addition of the GIA and the GSPC to the American State Department's list of "foreign terrorist organizations".

This erroneous interpretation was then taken up by the international community. From then on, the persistent violence of the Algerian armed groups, despite their small numbers, was explained by the fact that they had international support. Officially, these groups were reported to represent around 700 people in 2002 (as opposed to 30,000 between 1993 and 1996), split between several tendencies. According to General Maïza, "The GIA, under the leadership of Oukali Rachid known as Abou Tourab, comprises 60 units and are prevalent in the regions of Blida, Aïn Defla, Chlef, Médéa, Mascara, Sidi-Bel-Abbès and Skikda, acting in small groups of four to six people."[28] The GSPC was said to have around 300 fighters and to be active in the *wilayas* (provinces) of Tizi-Ouzou, Béjaïa, Batna, Tebessa and Jijel. Apart from these two groups, three Salafist-inspired armed formations involving around 300 individuals – Houmat Daawa Salafia, the Salafist Group for the *Jihad*, and the Fighting Salafist Group – were operating in the Mitidja. The spectacularly plummeting numbers can possibly be explained by the anti-terrorist policy (15,000 fighters killed by the security forces) and the effects of the clemency law under Liamine Zéroual (1995) and the law of 1999 on civil harmony which, as we said earlier, apparently prompted six thousand fighters to lay down their arms.

On relinquishing armed struggle, the Armée Islamique du Salut left the monopoly of the *jihad* to the groups inspired by a purely religious vision. Many observers see this as the explanation for the excesses of murderous violence in Algeria. In their view, the violence no longer had any political or strategic goal, but was based on a sectarian vision. The murdered women and children were the human sacrifices needed to bring about God's rule on earth.[29] The armed Islamists' orgies of violence are a fact, but the regime's demonization of the entire Islamist movement seems to have derived from a sense that the country was under a widespread curse: "dark forces" were said to have been unleashed on Algeria.

A sense of being cursed. The emergence of an eschatological or sectarian form of violence can only lead us to question the deeper causes of the violence that has been rampant in Algeria for some fifteen years: a protean violence that appears both in the natural world (floods, earthquakes) and in socio-political transformations (derailment of the electoral process in 1991-2, civil war, uprising in Kabylia). In other words, enlisting in sectarian armed movements in Algeria was now part of a local agenda where death and the quest for salvation occupied a huge place.

It might be useful to compare the map of violence to that of the civilian exodus. Around 1.5 million Algerians were forced to flee their villages between 1993 and 1997. Many villages were left deserted. Among the 1.5 million displaced persons, only 170,000 returned home following the promise that they would be protected by local defence groups. This exodus, linked to the past security situation, is part of a wider context of impoverishment. In its report entitled *Les effets du programme d'ajustement structurel sur les populations vulnérables*

[The effects of the structural adjustment programme on vulnerable sections of the population], published in 2000, the National Centre for Planning Research and Analysis reveals that 35% of the population is affected by poverty: i.e. out of 31 million Algerians, 12 million live on less than 18,000 dinars (180 euros) per annum. The economic reforms and the state's incompetence are largely responsible for this situation.

Amid these various ills, salvation was no longer sought through violence or through politics. This tragic decade seems to have witnessed the reappearance of intercessors[30] represented by the *marabouts*, or a withdrawal into the self. The sense of being doomed, which replaced the tendency to blame everything on colonialism, led to a multiple sense of anxiety. The quest for salvation went hand in hand with an individual search for redemption, as if the ills that had struck Algeria were all forms of divine punishment.

Throughout the 1990s, the Algerian Islamists very rarely resorted to suicide bombings. And yet there are numerous references to martyrs in Islamist literature and the *shahid* is a significant figure in the history of the War of Independence. So why this absence? First of all, confidence that the armed Islamist groups would defeat the regime led to a traditional guerrilla strategy. Above all, the would-be martyr seeks purity and entry to Paradise - he flees the real world, perceived as corrupt, unjust and unchangeable; and this search for another, supposedly better world did not in any way take hold of the Algerian Islamists' political *imaginaire*. On the contrary, their models of social success were the fighters in the War of Independence and the National Liberation Army. They remained convinced that it was possible to change the order here on earth as long as you were prepared to pay the price. Between 1989 and 1991, the FIS Islamists dreamed of transforming the Sahara into "California", and the armed groups wanted to turn Algeria into a revolutionary Islamic state capable of awakening a Muslim community which they saw as apathetic.

Secondly, the Algerian Islamists probably did not have the martyr's conviction that they would enter Paradise. Such a certainty is not automatic: the murder of civilians, especially Muslims, is strictly forbidden in Islam. If the Palestinian, Chechen and Kashmiri movements are able to justify this practice as the ultimate form of resistance against foreign occupation, in the case of Algeria this argument does not stand up. In short, for the Algerian Islamists, exercising violence against civilians was much more likely to arouse the fear of going to hell. This did not prevent the massacres, but it is worth noting that the attackers took care not to die during the operation, perhaps precisely for this reason. Lastly, the emergence of the suicide bomber reflects the imperious determination to draw a dividing line between a pure world and a corrupt world. In the case of Algeria, the Islamists rather swung between violence against others, compromise, denial and exile.

That said, three new factors now point to the likelihood of suicide bombings in Algeria: the armed groups no longer have confidence in the political struggle, which can result in "resistance" strategies that include this mode of action; the attacks of September 11 were a tremendous cause for celebration and are likely to lead to copycat attacks; and lastly, the worsening poverty creates favourable conditions for the agents of international networks seeking candidates for martyrdom. Are the Algerian Islamist movements in the process of swinging, like the Palestinian movements, from Islamic nationalism towards a strategy of terrorism based on suicide bombings? Such a swing generally assumes that other forms of action have been exhausted. The relative "recentness" of the Algerian conflict (compared with Palestine or Kashmir, for example) perhaps explains the "lateness" of this form of action. All the same, the lack of political vision or improvement in socioeconomic conditions provides fertile ground for the emergence of the suicide bomber, as has been shown in Morocco with the Casablanca bombing in May 2003.

7

THE STATE, POLITICAL ISLAM AND VIOLENCE: THE RECONFIGURATION OF YEMENI POLITICS SINCE 9/11

Ludmila du Bouchet

By posing a threat represented in radical existential terms and seemingly emanating from no singular source and devoid of address, September 11, as Der Derian correctly observes, has been taken out of the realm of politics and described as an exceptional event "beyond experience, outside of history and between wars", thereby positing "a world view of absolute differences in need of final solutions".[1] It has imposed an overarching reading of "terrorist" violence, with no discrete, discernable set of political demands presented, with no tangible and functional objectives to be attributed, all the more so as its religious character further blots out any known or recognizable rationale.[2] At the heart of this perceived new brand of violence, Islam (and the movements that go by that name) crystallizes as a defining feature in the form of a repeated articulation between Islamism and terror in American discourse. Indeed, "if the demise of the Soviet bloc can be said to have triggered a growing fixation on Islam as the object of post-Cold War ideological displacement…September 11th and the subsequent US-led "War On Terrorism" certainly sealed its fate as a main focus of intellectual and geo-strategic enquiry."[3]

Collapsing Yemen's "terrorist" image: a political process approach

It is in this broader international configuration that Yemen's present political transformations need to be situated. Yemen is frequently depicted as a quintessentially lawless country in which the state's writ is contested in large swaths of the territory. This image has been reinforced and even extended since 9/11, as Yemen has often been portrayed as a breeding ground for Islamist extremism. The seemingly endless armed clashes and hostage-taking, coupled with the porosity of the country's borders open to a manifold illegal trade in weapons and other prohibited goods, are widely regarded as evidence of the tenuousness of the state's authority and control. In addition, the series of attacks conducted by Islamists of one hue or another – the USS *Cole* bombing (12 October 2000), various attacks by the Sympathisers of Al-Qaida group (April 2002), the French *Limburg* oil tanker bombing (6 October 2002), the assassination of the Socialist leader Jarallah Omar (28 December 2002) followed by the murder of three American missionaries in Jiblah (30 December 2002) and various foiled attempts against Western premises (2003-2004) – have conjured up Yemen's dubious image as a potential "terrorist hub" or a hot spot of "Islamist violence".

For the US in particular, these various developments – especially the ongoing struggle to build and assert the central Yemeni state (a process itself predicated on success in meeting further challenges of socio-political and economic development), and the incidence of Islamist violence – have come increasingly since 9/11 to be subsumed under a single analytical and discursive rubric, that of the "Global War on Terror" (GWoT).[4] Thus, on the one hand, US counter-terrorist strategy is premised on the inadequacy of Yemen's "stateness", encapsulated in the image of "an impoverished hotbed of Muslim militancy and lawlessness".[5] On the other hand, tribal autonomy, the spread of weapons in the hands of tribesmen, the recurring practice of blocking roads, the kidnapping of foreigners, blowing up of oil pipelines, and suspected harbouring of Al-Qaida fugitives are all elements that are now seen to coalesce in a string of connotations.[6] Magnified and bundled together, these features have been construed as part of, and analogous to, the broad range of perceived threats in the GWoT, and treated accordingly.[7] Distinct issues, sites and processes – the USS *Cole* and *Limburg* bombings, kidnapping or murder of foreigners, as well as movements such as the Aden Abyan Islamic Army, Sympathisers of Al-Qaida, etc. – are equated and aggregated together into a homogeneous bloc, as manifestations of a unitary global threat, elevated to the status of paradigm: "Islamist terrorism". This all-encompassing designation conflates localized Islamist movements of varying ideological provenance and political purpose, and obscures the diverse political contexts and motivations that lie behind specific instances of "Islamist violence".

Similarly, by virtue of this articulation of danger, the challenges posed by the GWoT have highlighted the need to identify, circumscribe and re-territorialize the location of violence – violence that is held to be endowed precisely with a decentred, transnational, and multipolar outlook.[8] This reorientation has taken the form of a strategy aimed at "re-incarnating" the "terrorist threat" in the form of particular states with which it is associated, thus giving it an objective, defined and territorially contained quality. The state, and, along with it the powers and capabilities it is seen essentially to possess, has been reinstated as a matter of global significance and at the same time elicited as the relevant locus of counter-terrorist action.[9] By virtue of this equation, counter-terrorism in Yemen, and in particular the military build-up supported by the US and its Western allies, has translated into the reconstitution and consolidation of administrative and coercive apparatuses under the scheme of a broad "advice and support" mission.[10] This security agenda has been explicitly connected to the strengthening of state power in the pursuit of centralization, territorial control and outreach. In the process, US policy effectively reframes and subsumes the multi-faceted socio-political dynamics of Yemen – the evolving nature of the state, the tribal structure, the role of "Afghan" returnees, etc. – within a single over-arching discourse of counter-terrorism and security.

As a discursive and practical framework that acts as a powerful simplifying force, the "War on Terror" results in, and perpetuates unquestioned assumptions enshrined within the category of "Islamism" construed as an ideological monolith, intrinsically conducive to violence and ultimately geared towards political radicalization and revolutionary challenges to existing regimes. Further, to see Islamism through the "terrorist" lens leads to readings that are too often laden with representations coined in terms of social and political pathologies, even among the most renowned commentators on international affairs,[11] or else remain constrained by ideological determinants. This discursive approach and analytical perspective do far more to distort our understanding of Islamist violence in Yemen than to further it. For one thing, they dismiss the considerable variety of Yemeni Islamist movements that has already been comprehensively documented.[12] More specifically, easily blocked from view is the fact that the Yemeni Reform Grouping (the Islah party) comprises a multiplicity of internal dynamics and ideological sensitivities, making it the vehicle for infinitely diverse socio-economic demands that translate into changing political configurations, alignments and strategies.[13] By freezing the political, social and ideological dynamics of Islamism through purely endogenous and a-historical definitions that bring it to closure and treat it in isolation, such implicitly essentializing accounts fail to capture the complexity of what in fact is subject to profound debate and undergoes constant change integrally involving national and international developments.

In contradistinction to the aforementioned approaches, understanding Islamist movements requires examining their historical location and the manner of their insertion in particular social environments: that is, adopting a relational and dynamic perspective attuned to the mutually constitutive interaction between the external and the internal, to the intertwinings between historically changing transnational contexts and domestic socio-political orders.[14] Therefore, a political process explanatory framework can best account for the far-reaching transformations, in particular Islah's political reconfiguration, wrought by the GWoT in Yemen. Borrowing from Wiktorowicz's powerful demonstration, the concept of "political opportunity structure" sheds useful light on the way Islamist movements are embedded within broader social and political contexts marked by shifting sets of opportunities and constraints, and on the concomitant changes in strategic choices and doctrinal postures occurring in these movements in response.[15] Moving away from a purely endogenous perspective, political process explanations highlight structural elements such as access to and inclusion in political institutions and decision-making; a regime's openness and receptivity to demands expressed through institutional opposition; availability of peaceful avenues for political alternatives, coalition-building and alliance relationships; and the nature and level of state repression. Taken together, these elements are conceived as determining factors informing and actively shaping the Islamist movements' tactical considerations and their potential resort to violent contention.[16]

By the same token, far from merely forming a set of empirical circumstances - that is, an externalized dimension - international dynamics are constitutive of, and coeval with, the ways in which national opportunities and constraints crystallize in peculiar political configurations and alignments. External dynamics cannot be categorized as imported products superimposing themselves on pre-given, passive referent subjects – whether the state or society. They are reworked internally - that is, acted upon, appropriated and contested - as part and parcel of state formation in multiple and often paradoxical ways. Hence the novel strategies that the state deploys to accommodate, authorize and provide direction to complex global relations are inherently bound up with "domestic" social change.[17] The resulting context for thinking about the constitution and transformation of Islamist movements is located at the intersection of the local and the global, and forged out of contradictory state-society relationships, comprising at once confrontation, connection and interchange. In turn, an analysis that is cognisant of the significance of international dimensions, as formative of the wider dynamics to which Islamist movements respond and adjust, lays the groundwork for an enriched, comprehensive and multi-dimensional understanding of political opportunity structures and processes as larger encompassing fields of inter-relations.

Reconstituting state power in Yemen: a nexus of global and local dynamics

Yemen appears as a fruitful site for engaging with these problematics. It is distinguished by the thorough political, social, economic integration of Islamism by, and within, the state. For all the restrictions on the public sphere it currently witnesses, Yemen has preserved a measure of political openness and representational mechanisms warranting institutional inclusion and access to the legal political scene for the Islamist movement. This is in sharp contrast to what Burgat aptly terms the prevalent "Arab institutional norm" - that is, the disenfranchisement, criminalization and repression of significant political forces.[18] A strikingly original, and arguably commendable, feature of Yemen is that it has been able to eschew the political disruption and head-on confrontations that have often accompanied the emergence of Islamist trends elsewhere in the region.[19] Yemen's singularity with respect to the role and status of Islamists stems from both the permissive political context and liberalization that emerged in the wake of unification (1990) and the intricate and dynamic relationship historically entertained by the Republican regime with its Islamist counterparts.

Islah, "a formally institutionalised political party",[20] was created on 13 September 1990 as an offshoot of the ruling party, the General People's Congress (GPC), and is held to represent the Yemeni branch of the Muslim Brotherhood. Yet, in contrast to the static and over-ideologized image conveyed by the latter, Islah is best described as an inclusive, broad-based political movement with no definite unity or ideational cohesiveness. Amalgamating heterogeneous social, political and religious trends, Islah in effect inscribes the Muslim Brotherhood within a tribal, conservative coalitional framework. By dint of its internal diversity, Islah has demonstrated remarkable tactical and doctrinal flexibility in order to accommodate changing political conditions. Initially promoted and empowered as "a creature of the regime" in the context of a strategic partnership with the GPC, meant to provide a counterweight to the Yemeni Socialist Party (YSP),[21] Islah has been relegated to a posture of circumscribed opposition since the Socialist defeat, and its political leverage has been significantly eroded.

Yet although "decline" aptly describes this overall trend,[22] Islah's intertwining in multiple spheres with the regime of President Ali Abdullah Saleh, manifested in ruling elite constellations, belies any categorization in terms of binary confrontation. This manifold proximity, formalized in overlapping, intersecting networks of economic, political and ideological power relations, to use Micahel Mann's formulation, derives not only from the absence of ideological fault lines or violent political confrontation historically, but also from the crucial contribution of various Islamist forces to the establishment and consolidation of the Republican state. Hence, owing to the historical and ideological legitimacy vested in Islamist movements, Islah's pivotal role in structuring the Yemeni political landscape offers a significant point of departure from the general Arab picture – the latter typified by a vacuum or heavy restriction of political activity and participation and by the ensuing violent rejection of the existing order by the parties forced out of it.[23] By dint of both its internal composition and its interlocking with the regime, Islah forms one of the nexuses of relations that have crystallized into the fragile politico-territorial equilibrium at the core of Yemen's ongoing state formation.

Any analysis of the nature and role of Islamist violence in Yemen must be consistently referred back to this inclusive institutional framework. Equally important is the need to acknowledge the varied impacts of 9/11 as well as the significant social, political and military realignments and fissures they have translated into. These internal transformations reverberate on, and help define, changes in the substance and direction of the international security agenda in a recursive and mutually constitutive process. For all the struggles and tensions that have punctuated its turbulent history - both internal and those involving fellow Arab states such as Egypt and Saudi Arabia - Yemen was never the site of a thorough, intensive colonizing experience (except for the British settlement in Aden) nor of a direct and high-level Western presence or intervention. Although the all too common trope of Yemen's insulation and distinctiveness needs to be strongly qualified,[24] this historical feature lends particular salience to the far-reaching changes set in motion there by the GWoT.

As a marginal actor in international politics that came suddenly to the forefront of US preoccupations and turned into a frontline in the "War on Terror", Yemen has had little choice but to comply with US security injunctions, even when these threatened longstanding domestic social and political arrangements. Yet it has also proved itself to be far from a mere passive recipient of externally-imposed security policies. The Yemeni regime has sought actively to reassert the state, by assuming a central role in organizing, sanctioning and legitimizing the fight against terrorism. While the USS *Cole* attack was not viewed as an outright instance of "terrorism" or even as a criminal act, and indeed found enthusiastic support among the Yemeni public, the *Limburg* incident was unanimously condemned with vigour, Islamists included, and its consequences served to depict Yemen as "a victim of terrorism".[25] Both as a warship and as a symbol of the United States' heightened presence in Yemen and in the wider region - manifested by US use of Aden for naval refuelling on the way to and from the Gulf in the context of ongoing strikes and related sanctions on Iraq - the *Cole* was perceived as a military, hence legitimate target. In contrast, the attack on the *Limburg*, though linked to Yemen's international realignments in the wake of 9/11 and especially the ensuing crackdown on Islamist militants, was aimed at directly harming the government by targeting its economic interests. In addition to the loss of tourism revenue, port activity dropped owing to skyrocketing insurance premiums, which significantly eroded the profit margins the regime draws from oil exports and transshipment.[26]

Further, by mediating US security requirements, reappropriating them within an indigenous vocabulary and reformulating them according to national strategic priorities and its need for enhanced legitimacy, the Yemeni regime has exploited its position at the interface between the local and the international. This dynamic and adaptive stance is reflected in the official discourse, which has internalized the security argument while at the same time broadening its meaning and recasting it in the formal rhetoric of the restoration of public order, preservation of national interests and state consolidation.[27] The al-Huthi "rebellion" (2004-5), portrayed as "terrorism" with "foreign connections", provides a case in point for the proliferation of such representations.[28] Accusing al-Huthi of "treachery" and "backwardness" – seeking to overthrow the regime and the Republican legacy in order to restore the Imamate – the government resorted to indiscriminate repression and full military force to "quell" the movement.[29] As well as a performative discourse constitutive of political order, "terrorism" is operationalised as a perversion to be eliminated at all costs and articulates the injunction for a strong response. In turn, while condemning the "rebellion" in itself, the opposition, including Islah, uniformly adopted a critical, yet principled, stance, cast in legal and constitutional terms - a move for which it was charged with supporting the "rebels" and undermining "national unity".[30]

Therefore, the reconfiguration of Yemeni politics has been embodied most graphically in the significant shift in the historical relationship between the regime and the Islamists, most notably the Islah party: already under strain by early 2001, the relationship has been qualitatively recomposed at an accelerated pace under the impact of the post-9/11 US-led international security agenda. That said, even while responding comprehensively to US demands and adopting an overarching militarized strategy yielding repressive and exclusive trends, the Yemeni regime has largely resorted to its existing repertoire of negotiation, compromise and cooptation in dealing with domestic challengers. It has reformulated and adapted its stance rather than resorting to head-on confrontation. This framework of simultaneous accommodation, interaction and repression moreover explains why Islah has for its part elected to reconfigure itself in turn, and thus has enabled itself to remain part of the mainstream political arena as well as a key element in the institutional equation of Yemen.

Yemen and the Islamists: the state's trajectory

The Islamist socio-political component is central to Yemeni state and society realignments arising at the intersection of external and internal developments. The prevalent security theme, more precisely the "terrorist" label under which peculiar and distinct realities are bundled together in an essentialist manner, obfuscates such transformative processes by obliterating the longer-run history and the overall socio-political context in which the variegated strands of Islamism are woven together in complex and changing ways in Yemen. It obscures the historical setting in which Islamism has flourished concomitantly, and indeed inextricably, with Yemen's state trajectory. Conversely, to acknowledge the mutual constitution of the national and the international at work in the transformations brought about by the GWoT in Yemeni Islamist movements helps illuminate the totality of repressive measures and manifold societal bargains which they, simultaneously, are subjected to and act upon.

US policy seems strictly oriented towards the attainment of transnational security cooperation meant to ensure regional order and stability, and thus potentially able to remain independent from a fully political partnership. Yet, it has implications in Yemen that exceed the bounds of a strict focus on security. Reworked in a state still in its formative stage, security requirements ultimately assume a highly political dimension. Indeed, they are deliberately re-engineered by the regime according to its own logic, which recasts the international

security agenda in its specific terms, resulting in distinctive interpretations and implementations. The content bestowed by the Yemeni
government to the issue of international security is therefore a function of, and actively shaped by, internal power relations, strategic
domestic choices and political priorities. All of this deeply deflects
and alters the impact of a foreign policy orientation delineated and
imposed from outside and, concomitantly, refracted dynamically
through a process of domestication, through an endogenous usage.
Security partakes as much of a national project as of a process of globalization.

In effect the GWoT, coinciding with a narrowing of local political space, has prompted the Yemeni government to take repressive
measures against the majority of opposition forces. Yet, because of
the fragmented structure of political power, the regime enjoys incomplete dominance and its durability remains conditional on a game
of negotiated consensus building. Hence, the repression was engaged
gradually and selectively. It started with the most tangible targets,
that is, those potentially able to harm the regime directly – the "Arab
Afghans", the Islamic Jihad Movement, the Aden-Abyan Islamic Army
(AAIA) and Sheikh Abd al-Majid al-Zindani's radical component
within Islah[31]. It involved expulsion of hundreds of "illegal" foreign
students, closure of several schools suspected of harbouring radical
militants (al-Baihani school in Aden and the Dar al-Hadith institute
in Dhammaj, for instance),[32] monitoring of mosque sermons, a campaign of massive arrests among the "Afghan" veterans, strengthened
measures against "illegal immigrants",[33] and military operations (Jabal
Hatat in June 2003).

However, these processes should be referred back to the historical trajectory of enduring relations entertained by the Yemeni regime
with its newly defined targets. In the early 1990s, the bulk of the
returnees from the war in Afghanistan - thousands of Arabs, often
unwelcome in their own countries, as well as Yemeni militants led
by al-Zindani - found in Yemen a propitious sanctuary in which to

resettle. Their institutional and social integration derived from the 1994 civil war in which the Northern regime largely exploited the former "*mujahidin*", mobilizing them both militarily and ideologically against the Socialist, "atheist", so-called secessionists. Hence violent Islamist activism was tolerated and fostered by the state in the context of its mounting ideological rivalry with the Socialists.[34] As the outcome was the effective extension of the Northern power over its Southern counterpart, the "Afghan" support historically contributed to the consolidation of the victorious regime, which presented itself as the custodian of constitutionality, legality and unity.[35]

A few hundred of these "Afghans", both Yemenis and non-Yemenis, departed from the "normalization" path and formed new militant organizations - the Islamic Jihad Movement, which later split into the AAIA. The former, a loose guerrilla network, claimed responsibility for the kidnapping of tourists in 1998 and the attacks on the *Cole* and the *Limburg*.[36] However, as a means of both rewarding and controlling them, the majority of the "Afghans" were incorporated into the civil service, tribal affairs and military-security apparatuses, and politically absorbed into mainstream Islah. By dint of these inclusive and conciliatory social mechanisms, internal regulation of radicalization could be attained in Yemen in a manner unique in the region: "We used the dialogue method with them and tried to rehabilitate them so they can help develop the country".[37] Tariq al-Fadhli epitomizes these processes, from armed militancy to cooptation by the regime: a prominent "Afghan" and leader of the Islamic Jihad Movement, he then entered the President's tribe, Sanhan, by marriage, became the GPC representative in his home area, and now sits on the prestigious Shura Council.[38]

In a different fashion, the sporadic war waged since June 2004 against the al-Huthi "rebellion"[39] typifies the shifts in alliance strategies. From 1995 to 2001, the regime deliberately bolstered al-Huthi's Zaydi movement, later known as "Believing Youth", to counterbalance the implantation of Salafi and Wahhabi-inspired "scientific institutes" and mosques in the Northern area of Sa'ada. In addition to receiving political support for his educational activities, al-Huthi was tacitly allowed to raise the Islamic *zakat* tax and to establish a militia.[40] As the movement gained influence, it also became openly critical of government policies and cooperation with the US, in particular following the invasion of Iraq in 2003. The origins and causes of this confrontation are subject to differing interpretations; however, one can point to the various multi-level logics that have intersected it all along. Perceiving the movement as a challenge to its legitimacy, the state concurred with the US in its concerns about the dissemination of its defining slogan ("Death to America, Death to Israel, Long Life to Islam"). The military campaign might also have been the occasion to portray some senior military figures who led the operations and recruited tribal levies for this purpose, as the spearhead of the anti-terrorist struggle in Yemen and dispel US suspicions about their affinities with radical militants.[41] In the event, other local dynamics superimposed themselves on the existing national and international ones. The clashes that recurred in April and December 2005 had less to do with a beheaded ideological movement than with tribal unrest (inter-tribal disputes as well as state/tribes confrontations) in response both to the massive destruction, casualties and arrests that have punctuated this battle throughout and to promises of compensation and amnesty that were not kept by the authorities.[42]

The extension of repressive measures to encompass certain fringes of Islah - its Muslim Brotherhood component as well as al-Zindani's faction - needs to be situated within the longer-run of the regime's instrumentalization and repudiation of Islamist forces. Al-Zindani himself gained a seat on the Presidential Council (1993-97) only to end up earning a spot on the United Nations terrorist list and having his assets frozen under the US Treasury Department's blacklist in March 2004. This individual trajectory illustrates the convoluted history of the Islamist movement in Yemen. The latter has participated in its own right in the institutional system established by the

Republican regime from its outset, and is thus inscribed in its legal framework, but it now sees its positions increasingly eroded by the negative direction adopted under the guise of counter-terrorism - one that, overall, resorts more to repression than to politically inclusive means. Repression may very well be part and parcel of the state's legitimizing pronouncements and of the "fundamental choice" it took to side fully with the US-led "War on Terror". Nonetheless, the targets comprise social and political forces that belong to a legitimate, fully institutionalized party: Islah never framed its stance towards the state in anti-system terms or articulated a strategy of violent seizure of power. Furthermore, Islah's deliberate programmatic choice for the democratic system and pluralism has been demonstrated through the constitution of electoral platforms incorporating acceptance of institutionalized possibilities of government change and peaceful mobilization,[43] and in concrete terms through cabinet participation (1993-97) and opposition. This has contributed to the establishment of a political practice of legal opposition.[44] The intrinsic relationship of the Islamists with the regime – indeed Islah has often been referred to as "a party of the establishment centre" rather than as opposition[45] – means that global security changes, reverberated through the Yemeni political arena, can only precipitate alliance dislocations and a mixture of appropriation, reaction and adaptation of new political resources and ideas to local circumstances.

The intricate GPC-Islah relationship is at stake in this potentially unstable situation, resulting from the disruption of the "Yemeni institutional formula" founded hitherto on "forced participation" and "compulsory negotiation" between the state and the strong social forces that compose the political arena.[46] Indeed, far from falling within the familiar regime/opposition or power/counter-power analytical divide, these two main parties share a common ideological discourse and set of references. Their political practices overlap to a pronounced degree, and their rhetoric addresses the same constituency, which makes it difficult to draw precise lines between the two and their respective memberships and public audiences.[47] On only a few occasions has Islah been in clear opposition, for example during the 1991 referendum on whether or not to adopt the Shari'a as the sole, rather than main, source of law.

The blurring of party affiliations is further compounded by the fact that a number of Islah members have in the past been elected to Parliament under the GPC banner, and vice versa. It is epitomized by the prominent figure of Sheikh Abdullah bin Husayn al-Ahmar whose complex status - paramount Sheikh of the Hashid confederation from which President Saleh also originates, head of Islah and long-lasting Speaker of Parliament, irrespective of its overwhelming GPC majority – effectively cements the foundational alliance between the tribes, the Islamists and the regime.[48] The country's institutional pivot, Sheikh Al-Ahmar, is said to have "never cast a vote against the government", his "hand often raising the first in voting" in favour of a measure presented by the ruling party.[49] His own sons have been elected as both GPC and Islah MPs. This systematic alliance, in an unwritten understanding between President Saleh and Sheikh al-Ahmar to coexist politically so long as the status quo in terms of tribal privileges and patronage remains unchanged, derives from tribal, economic, and political interconnections and mutual strengthening that transcend any partisan cleavage.

This intertwining, taking the form of a kind of shared political board, flourishes in an environment marked by the primacy of Islam as the commonly assumed frame of reference among political and social forces, and thus displaying some ideological homogeneity: "In Yemen, Islam is not a cause of conflict.... . The Islamist project in Yemen is not owned by a distinct fraction or party, but it is the project and choice of the Yemeni people as a whole in its diverse components".[50] This is especially so since the 1994 war and the military and political defeat of Socialism, which, to some extent, brought to a close the era of ideologically motivated, "vertical" Islamist violence.[51] Muhammad al-Yadumi, Secretary General of Islah, is correct in observing that:

"There are no longer ideological or principled differences among the political forces themselves...The constitutional and legal situation in our country has made all people live within the same context."[52]

Because Islah is embedded within a broader social setting featuring a form of symbolical and normative uniformity – meaning that religion *per se* is not subject to contention – and because its Islamist component is incorporated into mainstream political structures pervaded by tribal affiliations, the growth of radical and anti-system Islamism has been inhibited and contained to a large extent. In particular, "tribal Islamism" and its ensuing pragmatism – by way of its proximity to the power centre and its integration within tribal society, military institutions and other social components – provides a counterbalance to potential religious contestation and accounts for Islah's limited proclivity for ideological radicalism.[53] Further, its loose ideological core allows Islah to nurture a wide array of political analyses, stances and trends, and to aggregate this diversity into a single party. As it is an assemblage bound together by a moderate and adapting strategy, its coherence rests upon "agreement on a minimum base", beyond which differences proliferate, leading to "complementarity rather than contradictions".[54] The flexible nature of Islah and, reciprocally, the GPC's political fluidity and absence of overriding ideological determinant help explain their interpenetration: "The style of politics in which Islah's leaders took part was that associated with the President's GPC, a style of patronage and connections rather than of ideology or of activists as vanguard of masses."[55]

At a deeper level, the composition of Islah and its multifaceted interlocking with the regime originate from the complex history of Yemen. Indeed, the Muslim Brotherhood has been historically associated with the construction of the Yemen Arab Republic and has contributed decisively to asserting the Northern regime's authority and the legitimacy. This trajectory goes back to the 1962 revolution and the ensuing civil war, in which a landmark was Muhammad Zubayri's foundation of a "Hizb Allah" (along with al-Zindani) in order to create a broad receptacle for republican political mobilization. This made it possible to strike an alliance with the leading sheikhs of the Hashid and Bakil tribes. While providing the Islamist movement with solid anchorage in the most influential and enduring social forces and with decisive public implantation, this tactical move of rallying the tribes around the republican flag, and securing their long-lasting allegiance to the regime, confirmed the Islamists as one of its fundamental pillars.[56]

This was compounded by the spearhead role played by the Islamist movement as a whole, ranging from part of the Muslim Brotherhood to armed activists (including some of the Salafiyya), in the proactive confrontation with the Socialists before and during unification, and again at the time of the 1994 civil war. The consolidation of Saleh's regime occurred against a backdrop of armed struggles in which the Islamists' close ties to the Northern elite and their hostile ideological stance made it possible for them to be harnessed repeatedly to counter Socialist challenges. This was evidenced by the decisive role played by the Islamic Front in helping the North defeat the southern-based left-wing guerrilla resistance of the National Democratic Front (1979-82),[57] as well as by the campaign of assassination of Socialist leaders around the time of unification and the subsequent "transitional period", reaching a final stage in the form of a *jihad* against the "unbelieving", "separatist" South in 1994.[58] This historical trajectory, and the deep-rooted legitimacy acquired by Islamists as a consequence, explain why they never were intent on a revolutionary challenge to the existing political order. As a political organization, Islah never articulated violent Islamist contention as a strategy *per se,* although it was actively supported by some of its members.[59] Rather, as part and parcel of Yemen's distinctive institutional transaction, Islamist violence was authored, deliberately organized and channelled by the regime towards its own assertion and, thus, became key to its constitution, reproduction and transformation. Al-Yadumi, again, usefully summarizes the issue:

"We have been active even before the emergence of the GPC and we have contributed to its establishment. We also have taken part in formulating its political platform...the National Charter. The history of this country has not witnessed a single act of political violence from our side. It is true that we took up arms in the early 1980s – in 1981 and 1982 – in the face of Communist expansion to stop it in the Northern Yemeni governorates. But this was with the Yemeni Armed Forces in one trench, led by the President of the Republic."[60]

Thus the GPC, and in particular President Saleh, owe much historically and ideologically to the Islamist movement, whose own strength derives from the fact that it has long been a bulwark of the regime.

Re-ordering political relations: a dual strategy of repression and accommodation

Yemen, a country "socially and politically...full of 'articulations' and balances and counterbalances", rests on a set of complex accommodations and interactions involving continuous negotiation and compromise, to the extent that, in the face of various countervailing forces, "the state in many ways 'complements' rather than 'contradicts' society".[61] The concrete implementation of American security exigencies has made possible an unprecedented strengthening of Yemen's weak central government and consolidation of the regime's power, in particular the bolstering of the ruling party's political dominance in the name of preventing "a second Afghanistan". The nature of this statist assertion is best described as an intensification of extant trends within the regime, mainly political preservation. But its factual manifestations reveal qualitative changes: "9/11 was not a compelling factor but it created a political space...the government is writing the security issue to retreat from democratization and gain more latitude."[62] With respect to the Islamists, and within the context of both political inclusion and social interpenetration with the regime, the irruption of US-led external demands, stemming from a specific articulation of danger, clad in absolute terms - "terrorism" or "extremism" - has triggered effects of political polarization, fragmentation, and recomposed alliances.

The international context, and its primary focus on the designation and eradication of the "terrorist" menace identified with the Islamist movement in general, coincides locally with the efforts engineered by the regime to curb its main challenger, Islah, and to relegate it to a role of tame opposition. For the Yemeni regime, US pressures on the international security front are as much a constraining factor (to avoid repeating the 1990 "error")[63] as a structure of opportunity and an added justification for furthering an internal political reordering and tightening its domestic grip at the expense of its former strategic ally. A process set in motion since the failure of the unionist pact with the South in 1994 is thus coming to completion. The military defeat of the YSP, and its related disappearance from the political scene, eliminated the regime's need to maintain a strategic alliance with Islah to offset its Socialist counterpart. By the same token, this nullified the rational calculus underlying the endorsement of political and institutional pluralism. The resulting limitations of political space, bound up with the growing dominance of the GPC, coincided with the decline of Islah's political power and influence as a party from 1995 onwards.[64]

By early 2001, changes in the national and international context, and the strategies elicited by the government in response, had led to a significant deterioration in the GPC/Islah relationship. The shift into opposition by Islah, and the ensuing bitter contest during the February 2001 local elections, combined with mounting US pressure to produce a clampdown on Islamist militants following the USS *Cole* attack, gave the government the necessary political leeway to implement the 1992 education law integrating all schools and curricula, including the Islah-run network of "scientific institutes", into a unified public scheme. This amounted to a major blow for Islah, whose educational activities – in effect its social, religious and political recruitment base – had been tolerated so far as a token of government appreciation of its support in the 1994 war.[65] The discursive economy of "terrorism" has provided the GPC with further resources to disparage and contain

Islah. The white paper on security strategy, submitted to the Parliament by Prime Minister Ba-Jammal in early 2003, accused opposition parties (implicitly, Islah) of having links with terrorist organizations or individuals,[66] thereby announcing the tone of the subsequent 2003 electoral campaign which saw the "terrorism" label overused to undermine the opposition.[67]

In a tactical move to mitigate its increasing institutional relegation, Islah banded with a cohort of parties in an opposition coalition, the Joint Meeting Parties (JMP),[68] designed as a united front to counteract the ruling party in the 27 April 2003 parliamentary elections. In the context of this recomposed political picture, the representational and political practices that crystallize around the security referent encouraged a process of differentiation and polarization that serves the government strategy to fragment the opposition bloc and exploit rifts between Islah's moderate and radical wings.[69] The JMP were notably impaired by the assassination of the YSP deputy secretary-general Jarallah Omar while addressing the Islah party congress and calling for the unification of Islamist and Socialist forces to further democratization, and by the ensuing accusations levelled at Islah: it achieved mixed results in coordinating electoral pacts involving the withdrawal of candidates. Islah won overwhelmingly in urban areas and secured significant electoral districts, but the elections confirmed its retreat.[70] Conversely, they consolidated GPC hegemony, hailed as the epitome of "centrism, moderation and care for national unity", by giving it an absolute majority, and hence total control of state agencies.[71] By evicting Islah from state and administrative structures and restricting its participation on the political stage, the government has effectively marginalized it. In the light of this constriction, Yemen's political profile seems to bear a growing similarity to that of fellow Arab states – "a one-party quasi-democracy…wherein opposition parties are allowed to compete but not to win".[72]

However, to speak of Saleh's regime in terms of unfettered control over Yemeni politics would misrepresent the issue. Rather, the

GPC/Islah disjunction has generated recomposed political alliances. For all its enhanced capacity and its manifest solidification, the regime enjoys only partial legitimacy and remains dependent on its ability to strike bargains with plural social forces. It operates not only in a country marked by an incomplete process of national integration and a segmented political order, but also amidst the heightened tensions sparked by its broad amenability to US security demands. The politics of regime survival impose a balancing act that precludes an outright break with the pattern of incremental change and negotiated consensus-building that has historically prevailed in Yemeni political life and thereby ensured the regime's enduring stability. Originally created in 1982 as a loosely defined forum gathering Saleh's multiple strands of support in one umbrella organization, the GPC is distinguished by its flexible, non-confrontational political style. Indeed, as a continued effort to restructure politics towards national consensus, the GPC still rules by incorporating a wide array of interests and groups from nearly the entire political spectrum. Thanks to its key role in channelling access to public positions and resources, it has been able to mobilize both conservative and modernist-technocratic figures, and to repeatedly co-opt large swaths of the opposition.[73] "Shoring up the center and extending support"[74] remains Saleh's overall approach to domestic politics and his strategy to increase state legitimacy.

For all its exclusive and repressive connotations, US-led "counter-terrorism" has translated into distinctive arrangements and compromises when blended with the relational style of Yemeni domestic politics and inscribed within the broad national-popular image conveyed by the regime as the repository of the legitimizing myth of Yemeni unity. In the wake of the US drone attack (5 November 2002) and the national uproar that followed, President Saleh performed a much publicized pilgrimage to Mecca, accompanied by Sheikh al-Ahmar and Sheikh al-Zindani, thereby reasserting Yemen's tribal and religious cohesion. Moreover, a Dialogue Committee, headed by Judge al-Hitar, was established to meet detainees (including "Afghans" and

members of the AAIA) with the objective of persuading them to re-
nounce their radical views.[75] This reformist gesture was accompanied
by a call upon the *ulema* to declare "fanaticism and extremism ... sinful
when they undermine the security and stability of the homeland".[76]
360 prisoners were released on bail and socially rehabilitated between
autumn of 2002 and winter 2005. In the same vein, the government
launched a full-scale military operation led by Special Operations
Forces in Jabal Hatat in June 2003, in a crackdown on some 80 radical
activists drawn from the remnants of the AAIA and Islamic Jihad.[77]
A high point in repression, this event paradoxically unfolded with
the negotiated surrender of the group's leader, Khaled al-Nabi, who
was granted presidential pardon and some privileges, along with his
brother and several followers, after repenting.[78] In effect, the regime
pursues a dual strategy both towards its domestic constituency – to
demonstrate its ability to negotiate and act regardless of US concerns[79]
– and towards the international community, to show its commitment
to human rights and improve its image abroad. Although its efficacy
is questionable,[80] this accommodation policy is unintelligible without
reference to the primary political issue, the nature of the Yemeni state
and its survival through continuous compromise among a plurality of
interests.

The regime's malleability allows the reconfiguration of the Yemeni transactional formula to take unexpected and sinuous paths. The
dynamic reshuffling of political alliances spurred by the international
context has prompted the authorities to make significant conciliatory
moves across the whole political and ideological spectrum. While
granting amnesty to 16 exiled Socialist leaders in the name of the
need for all forces to participate in nation building,[81] the regime continues to draw selectively on religious forces in order to bolster its
legitimacy. In effect, the GPC's ideological looseness, its long lasting
proximity to Islah, and the primacy of Islam as the defining frame of
reference across society are concurrent elements making it easy for
the regime to appropriate Islah's religious field of discourse. It fosters

a literalist, quiescent version of Islam in order to curb the Muslim Brotherhood's political breakthrough. The regime has turned the apolitical Salafi trends into "objective allies": it encourages their doctrinal stance prohibiting electoral participation and advocating abstention, to divide the Islamist movement from within and lessen Islah's gains.[82] Likewise, in the context of the ongoing clashes with the Zaydi "Believing Youth", labelled as a "confessional sedition" and "religious deviance", the regime promotes their ideological adversaries, the Salafis, who appear to have taken advantage of the government's recent decision to close down all "unlicensed" religious institutions – in effect, often Zaydi schools.[83]

The difficult political re-foundation of Islah

Islah finds itself at a critical juncture marked by "an intensely negative international environment"[84] and the correlated internal restrictions imposed on political participation. However, the conjunction of US security concerns with the regime's own political agenda has not only reinforced the ruling party and driven it towards marginalizing Islah by highlighting its supposed "terrorist links". It has also precipitated internal realignments, compelling Islah to make discursive and strategic adjustments in a pragmatic move congruent with the trajectories of the Egyptian and Turkish branches of Muslim Brotherhood. Perceiving the necessity to adapt to the "domestication of an exogenous, international vocabulary", and choosing accommodation rather than confrontation with the regime, Islah has reviewed its stances and reformulated its speeches away from its religious emphasis: "The US-Yemeni security cooperation is not weakening Islah as much as changing it".[85] For instance, it immediately condemned the 9/11 attacks and officially distanced itself from them.[86] More recently Islah has voiced public support for US President Bush's Greater Initiative for the Middle East and his call for democratic reforms.

Instances of violence emanating from Islamist elements and their interpretive refraction within Islah provide a useful entry point into

the party's transformative dynamics. The assassination of YSP leader
Jarallah Omar had a critical impact, further compounded by the following attack on three American missionaries at the Baptist Hospital of
Jiblah. The Interior Minister claimed that Omar's murderer, Ali Jarallah, an "Afghan" veteran and a student of al-Iman University, had been
a member of Islah, like his colleague involved in the Jiblah incident.[87]
According to Islah, because they were exploited by the government to
confine Islamists to "the extremist stereotype", both events assumed
a political meaning ("political assassinations") and were read as a dual,
joint attempt to jeopardize the party's reformist transition.[88] They occurred in the context of a major political refashioning, as the nascent
JMP, though blending together heterogeneous "parties which never
truly stood in opposition to the GPC, but rather fought each other",
gathered momentum in advance of the 2003 parliamentary elections,
a process in which the leading figure of Omar was instrumental.[89]
Taking place at a time when Islah's political *infitah*, both internal and
external, reached its climax and the party sought to convey an image
of moderation and tolerance to its domestic constituency, its political
partners (especially the YSP) and the international community, the
two murderous acts were perceived as an attack emanating from
within, and directed against the party *per se*.[90] The first one, "an in-
ward strike", was designed to rivet domestic attention on Islah's radical trends, away from its political renovation process, and to foil the
joint opposition framework.[91] In turn, the Jiblah incident contributed
to the dissemination of negative representations of Islah as inherently
anti-Western and ideologically fanatical to the outside world.[92]

These challenges were a serious blow to the JMP's cohesion, with
the potential to disrupt it altogether. Yet, ultimately they gave additional impulse to, and reinforced, Islah's determination to further
the opposition coalition beyond the short-term, strategic calculus
that originally informed it. Its liberal wing, embodied by Muhammad
Qahtan, head of the political committee, and by secretary-general
Muhammad al-Yadumi, strives to refigure Islah as a full-fledged po-

litical party – and not simply an Islamist movement – by shifting its self-definition and stances away from its ideological, doctrinaire underpinnings ("Islam is the solution") to a genuinely political content.[93] This was evidenced by its 2003 electoral programme, centred on socio-economic issues and notably purged of Islamic religious references.[94] In this light, the fiery speeches of al-Zindani and his radical faction against the return of the amnestied Socialists appeared to serve the regime rather than his own party.[95] In effect, al-Zindani needs Saleh's protection both to preserve his economic assets and his institutional base, al-Iman University, and to shield him from recurring US pressure. In return, Saleh is dependent upon al-Zindani to keep his followers in check and ensure their support for the regime.[96]

More importantly, by publicizing radical positions, al-Zindani's group undermines the party and smothers its reformist endeavours. Acting as an obstructive force from within, it confines the party to "inherited" ideological positions, inhibits its renovation and effectively prevents it from gaining political ascendance, all of which benefits the regime.[97] For instance, Islah's commendable endorsement of women's electoral candidacy and participation in politics – a pragmatic move meant to attract a substantial, long neglected pool of voters and to improve outside perceptions of the party – was vehemently condemned both by al-Zindani's faction and by the GPC.[98] Caught between the harsh criticism articulated by its radical wing and the reappraisal by the GPC – adept at using al-Zindani's communiqués in order to brand Islah's moves as, depending on the circumstances, either encouraging "terrorism" or "betraying the nation" – Islah is forced to react defensively in order to rectify its distorted image.[99] While al-Zindani's relative decline since his US indictment in 2004 has created an opportunity to tip the internal balance in favour of the reformist grouping, the latter, if not totally cornered, is somehow politically paralyzed by all these developments and by the party's structure of power.

Not only does the ruling party often outmanoeuvre it, but the JMP also has yet to prove its ability to stage itself as an effectual and cohesive opposition force and to present a valid alternative political platform.[100] This in turn hinges on Islah's will and capacity to overcome its historical reluctance to relinquish its strong relationship with the GPC and to turn into an effective opposition party. As prominent figures in the ruling elite, Islah leaders partake as much of the opposition's as of the regime's equation, all the more as both sides are often interlocked in business activities.[101] For instance, the party derives its institutional strength and internal cohesion from Sheikh al-Ahmar's unique pivotal position and close personal ties with the President; yet this systematic inter-elite alliance also constrains Islah from within and hinders it from emerging as a freestanding political force. This issue has sparked off infighting. Spurred by the defection of both radicals opposed to internal reforms and liberals breaking ranks to join the GPC, debates have focused on internal democratization, notably decision-making processes, promotion procedures (voting vs. top-down appointment) and tolerance of internal dissent. Opposing the "autocratic structure" of the party, based on principles of "obedience and unquestionable loyalty to its leaders", young members call for their political ambitions and critical assessments to be taken into account.[102] In effect, the issue of reforms partially coincides with generation-based, intra-party fissures between a leadership keen on preserving Islah in its existing format, both internally and with respect to the GPC, and an intellectual new guard aspiring to refashion it into a distinctively political party.

Conclusion

The issue of "terrorism", engineered as an "organizing principle"[103] for US thinking and action in various arenas, has implications in Yemen that are unintelligible outside a perspective that simultaneously addresses their distinct local political and historical context and situates them in their relevant global setting. In Yemen, as elsewhere, the efficacy of 9/11 as the anchor of a legitimating narrative for the crackdown on Islamists and domestic "subversion" has been largely demonstrated. Yet, far from precipitating the kind of processes depicted by Henry and Springborg's inclusion of Yemen in the category of "bunker states" – that is, "praetorian republics [ruling] physically or metaphorically from bunkers...in a potential state of war with [their] societies"[104] – the GWoT has prompted a political and institutional reordering running the full gamut from local arrangement, mediation and retribution, to opposition and resistance. In effect, in a state whose social contract and legitimacy are still very much open to negotiation, and where state monopoly over the legitimate use of violence has not been achieved, Yemeni-US security cooperation is problematic. The regime, though notably strengthened and less dependent than in the past on resorting to alliances to ensure its survival, is still forced to strike bargains and compose with the various social and political forces that stand in counterpoise to state authority. Stemming from the segmented socio-territorial structure of power, this necessary balancing act, and President Saleh's artful ability to "divide and rule" as much as to compromise and co-opt, account for the regime's resilience as well as the preservation of a margin of political space and expression.

In effect, for all the violence emanating from various sides, including the state, since 2001, Islah, and the Islamists as a whole, are still integral to the legitimation and stability of the regime. Islamism in Yemen cannot be construed as an internal threat, as prone to confrontation with the state. Hence, while substantially reducing Islah's manoeuvrable space, in edging away from a purely security-oriented strategy, the regime has generally engaged it through a complex and contradictory political dynamic that exemplifies Yemen's "state of negotiations". In turn, Islah's political pragmatism has enabled it to adjust continuously to a changing domestic and international environment. Though more acutely divided, the political landscape has not become polarized violently. The intermingled relationships and fluid alliances that weave Yemen's political fabric introduce constraints on state authoritarianism. Yet, while Yemen remains "unique in the region in [its] need for civil society",[105] the very reasons that preclude its evolution into a dictatorship also hamper its democratization. As has been shown, Yemen's multiple counterbalancing influences consist as much of a limit placed on the state's centralizing and autocratic trends as of a constraining factor mitigating against the development of significant alternative opposition forces.

NOTES

INTRODUCTION: *IMAGINAIRES* OF ISLAMIST VIOLENCE

[1] Frédéric Encel, *Géopolitque de l'Apocalypse: la démocratie à l'épreuve de l'islamisme*. Paris: Flammarion, 2002 is a prize example of a culturalist approach overflowing with the sense of a clash of civilizations.

[2] Alexandre Del Valle, researcher at the International Institute of Strategic Studies, interview, *Le Figaro*, 25 September 2001.

[3] Alfred Morabia, *Le Gîhad dans l'Islam médiéval* , Paris, Albin Michel, 1993, p. 342.

[4] Quintan Wiktorowicz, ed., *Islamic Activism. A Social Movement Theory Approach*. Bloomington: Indiana University Press, 2004.

[5] Bernard Lewis, "What Went Wrong?" *The Atlantic Monthly*, Vol. 289, no. 1, January 2002; *Western Impact and Middle Eastern Response*, Oxford University Press, 2002.

[6] Jean-Paul Charnay, *L'Islam et la guerre: de la guerre juste à la révolution sainte*, Paris, Fayard, 1986..

[7] *L'islamisme en face*, Paris, La Découverte, 2004.

[8] Anthony H. Cordesman wrote, "The Bush Administration has touched upon all these issues in its call for democracy in the Arab world, but the end result has been slogans rather than substance...The end result is that the Administration's efforts have generally appeared in the region to be calls for regime change favourable to the US, rather than support for practical reform". "The Transatlantic Alliance: is 2004 the year of the Greater Middle East?" in CSIS. ORG.

[9] "In a matter of only a few years, Palestine will be one of two new Arab democratic states. The other neonatal Arab democracy will be Iraq. These

unthinkable developments will revolutionize the power dynamic in the Middle East, powerfully adding to the effects of the liberation of Afghanistan to force Arab and Islamic regimes to increasingly allow democratic reforms. A majority of Arabs will come to see America as the essential ally in progress toward liberty in their own lands". Michael Kelly, *Washington Post*, 26 June 2002. See "Democracy Mirage in the Middle East", Carnegie Endowment For International Peace, October 2002.

10 Daniel Brumberg, *Moyen-Orient: l'enjeu démocratique*, Paris, Michalon, 2003.

11 Of Albanian origin, theologian Al Albani is considered a Salafist. He studied in Syria and taught at the Islamic University of Medina. "Attentats suicides dans la balance de la loi islamique", http://www.sounnah.free.fr/dawah_attentat_albani.htm

12 Ibn Taymiyya, in Henri Laoust, *Le Traité de Droit public d'Ibn Taymiyya*, Beirut, Institut français de Damas, 1948, p. 28.

13 *Al Sharq Al Awsat*, 21 April 2001.

14 Cited by Rasha Saad, "Weapons of the weak", *Al Ahram Weekly* Online, 13-19 December 2001.

15 Al Qaradawi, Egyptian theologian and Dean of the College of Sharia and Islamic Studies and director of the Centre for Sunna and Sirah at the University of Qatar. 2 March 2003, "Le martyr et l'expiation des péchés", http://www.islamophile.org/spip/article555.htm

16 Olivier Roy, *L'islam mondialisé*, Paris, Seuil, 2002, pp. 162-3.

17 Diego Gambetta, ed., *Making Sense of Suicide Missions*. Oxford University Press, 2005.

18 R. Pape, "The Strategic Logic of Suicide Terrorism", *American Political Science Review*, vol. 97, N° 3, August 2003.

19 Pape considers that Al-Qaida also has a territorial demand in stipulating the departure of American troops from Saudi Arabia.

20 See Fethi Benslama, *La psychanalyse à l'épreuve de l'islam*, Paris, Aubier, 2002.

21 Scott Atran, "Combating Al-Qaida's splinters", *Washington Quarterly*, vol. 27, n° 3, p.65-113.

22 Laurens Henry, *Le grand jeu: Orient arabe et rivalités internationales depuis 1945*, Paris, Colin, 1991.

23 "Moi, Khaled Kelkal", *Le Monde*, 7 October 1995.

24 Marc Sageman, *Understanding Terror Networks*, Philadelphia, University of Pennsylvania Press, 2004.

[25] According to Nasra Hassan who interviewed 250 would-be suicide bombers and recruiters in the Gaza Strip: "An arsenal of believers", *The New Yorker*, 19 November 2001.

[26] Gilles Kepel stresses: "the *ulema* of modern Islam have lost control of the unleashing of the jihad , no longer have the means to warn the believers of the advent of the *fitna*: they have been overtaken by militant activists who mock their guile, are deliberately ignorant of the long history of Muslim societies..." in *Fitna. Guerre au cœur de l'islam*, Paris, Gallimard, 2004, p. 336.

[27] Particularly in *Suicide Bombers: Allah's New Martyrs*, trans. David Macey, London, Pluto Press, 2004.

[28] This concept, put forward by the sociologist Charles Tilly, designates the means at the disposal of a protesting group to achieve its shared aims (plane hijacking, mutiny, the breaking of machinery, disruption, village battles, rebellions against taxes, hunger riots, collective self immolation, lynchings, vendetta, petitions, strikes, demonstrations, etc.). Charles Tilly, *From Mobilization to Revolution*, Reading, MA, Addison-Wesley Publishing Company, 1978, p. 151.

[29] Joyce M. Davis, *Martyrs. Innocence, Vengeance and Despair in the Middle East*, Basingstoke: Palgrave, 2003.

[30] Mohammed M. Hafez, *Why Muslims Rebel. Repression and Resistance in the Islamic World*, London, Lynne Rienner Publishers, 2003.

[31] This was the case of the suicide bombing against the Parliament in New Delhi in December 2001, which the authorities still attribute to a Pakistani jihadist organization (the Jaish-i-e Muhammad). A member of this organization claimed responsibility for it independently (motivated by the rivalry between jihadist organizations), but he was vehemently contradicted by his hierarchical superiors the following day.

[32] "The targeted use of self-destructive human beings against a group perceived as the enemy, for political ends". Cf. Riaz Hassan, "Suicide Attacks. Life as a Weapon", ISIM *Newsletter*, n°14, June 2004, p. 8.

[33] See the chapter by Hamidi Redissi and Jan-Erik Lane in this book.

[34] Gilles Kepel, *Jihad. The Trail of Political Islam,* London, I.B. Tauris, 2004.

[35] Rik Coolsaet, *Le mythe al Qaida: le Terrorism symptôme d'une société malade,* Bierges, Belgium, 2004, 168 p.

[36] Pénélope Larzillière, "Le "martyr" palestinien, nouvelle figure d'un nation-alisme en échec", in Alain Dieckhoff and Rémy Leveau, eds, *Israéliens et Palestiniens: la guerre en partage*, Paris, Balland, 2003.

[37] Michel Wieviorka, *The Making of Terrorism*, University of Chicago Press, 1993, p. 64.

[38] J-F.Bayart, *The Illusion of Cultural Identity*, London, Hurst, 2005, p. 137.

[39] H. Bozarslan, *Violence in the Middle East: From Political Struggle to Self Sacrifice*, Princeton, Markus Wiener Publishers, 2004.

1. DOES ISLAM PROVIDE A THEORY OF VIOLENCE?

[1] Carl Schmitt, *The Concept of the Political*, trans. George Schwab, University of Chicago Press, 1996, p. 49. See Leo Strauss on this concept in Carl Schmitt, *The Crisis of Parliamentary Democracy*, trans. Ellen Kennedy, Cambridge, MA, MIT Press, 1988.

[2]. The English version of the passages quoted from the Koran are taken from *The Holy Koran*, rev. trans. and ed. Ali Abdullah Yusuf, Beltsville, MD, Amana Publications, 1989.

[3] Tabari, *Chronique* (in Arabic), 1958, vol. 1, pp. 608-614. See an outline of the facts in *Chronique de Tabari*, trans. Zotenberg, Paris, Maisonneuve, vol. 3, pp. 68-72.

[4] Jean Leca and Yves Schmeil, "Clientélisme et néopatrimonialisme dans le monde arabe", *International Political Science Review*, 4, 1983, p. 4.

[5] Louis Massignon, *Opera Minora*, Beirut, Dâr al-Ma'âref, 1963, vol. 2, p. 305.

[6] See the minutes of the hearing edited by Rifaat Sayed Ahmed, *The Militant Prophet*, London, Riad El-Rayyes, vol. 1, 1999.

[7] F. Khosrokhavar, "Iran: de la revolution à l'islamisme hezbollah" in Gilles Kepel, ed., *Les politiques de Dieu*, Paris, Seuil, 1989. By the same author, *L'islam et la mort*, Paris, Harmattan, 1995.

[8] For an excellent analysis of religious sedition that has driven terrorists to at-tack new targets, see Alain Roussillon, "Changer la société par le jihad" in *Le phénomène de la violence*, Les Cahiers du CEDEJ, Cairo, 1994, pp. 295-319.

[9] Gilles Kepel, *La revanche de Dieu*, Paris, Seuil, 1991, p. 72.

[10] I. Goldziher, *Muslim Studies*, London, George Allen & Unwin, 1967, vol. 1, ch. 1 ("Muruwa and dîn"), pp. 11-44.

[11] Alfred Morabia, *Le Gîhad dans l'Islam médiéval*, Paris, Albin Michel, 1993, ch. 7, in particular pp. 211-14.

12 See in particular the influence of the Crusades on the contemporary Arab mind in E. Sivan, *Mythes politiques arabes*, Paris, Fayard, 1995, ch. 1, pp. 23-65.

13 The most famous were Count Raymond II of Tripoli and Syria, killed in 1129 or 1130 and Conrad, Marquis of Montferrat, killed in Tyre in 1192.

14 As happened with for Louis IX (Saint Louis) and the German emperor Frederick II.

15 Morabia, *Le Gîhad dans l'Islam médiéval*, p. 304.

16 Algeria, Saudi Arabia, Bahrain, Egypt, Jordan, Kuwait, Morocco, Somalia, Libya, Tunisia, and Yemen.

17 Mohamed Kerrou, "Blasphème et apostasie en Islam" in *Monothéismes et modernités*, Tunis, OROC/Friederich-Naumann, 1996, pp. 117-204.

18 See I. Leverrier, "Le FIS entre la hâte et la patience" in G. Kepel, ed., *Les politiques de dieu*, (note 7), pp. 45-6.

19 See the translation of his testimony in *Maghreb Machrek*, no. 141, 1993, p. 123.

20 William O. Beeman, "Terrorism: Community Based or State Supported?", *Arab-American Affairs*, no. 16, Spring 1986, pp. 29-36, where it is defined as consisting of four elements: illegal acts; against defensive targets; for political ends; and unacceptable by other criteria. See also Walter Laqueur, *Terrorism*, London, Weidenfeld and Nicolson, 1977, pp. 7 and 79.

21 Laqueur (note 20), pp. 3-20; in the same spirit but with the addition of constant analogies with previous historical events, see also Franklin L. Ford, *Le meutre politique: Du tyrannicide au terrorisme*, Paris, PUF, p. 346.

22 Ford (note 21), chapters 1-8.

23 Louis Gardet, *Les homes de l'islam*, Paris, Hachette, 1977, p. 76. See also Roger Brunshvig, *Etudes d'islamologie*, Paris, Vrin, 1977, vol. 1, p. 180.

24 Henri Corbin, *Trilogie ismaélienne*, Paris, Maisonneuve, 1961, vol. 3, pp. 3-23.

25 Mohamed S. Ashmawy, "Terreur et terrorisme au Moyen Orient", in *Contre l'islamisme*, Paris, La Découverte, 1990, p. 74.

26 Bernard Lewis, "Licence to Kill", op. cit., p. 19.

27 James A. Bill & Carl Leiden, *The Middle East: Politics and Power*, Boston, Allyn and Bacon, 1974. See in particular the list of 20th century assassinations between 1918 and 1973, p. 216.

28 On Hezbollah, see Olivier Carré, "Quelques mots clefs de Muhammed Husayn Fadhlallah", CERI, 1987. See also D. Krämer, "La morale du Hezbollah et sa logique", *Maghreb Machrek*, Jan.-Mar. 1988, pp. 39-59.

29 The most recent condemnation was that made by the heads of state of the Arab League following the September 11 tragedy. But such condemnations are by no means general. The disapproval expressed by "higher ups" does not do away with the ambiguity that we have analyzed, namely the distinction to be made between terrorism and legitimate violent action.

30 Robin Wright, *The Sacred Rage*, New York, Linden Press/Simon and Shuster, 1985, p. 41. 31. J. Wellhausen, *Das arabische Reich und sein Sturz*, Berlin, Walter de Gruyter, 1960 [1909].

32 Pier-Cesare Bori, *L'interprétation infinie*, Paris, Cerf, 1991.

33 G.E. Von Grunebaum, *Medieval Islam: A Study in Cultural Orientation*, University of Chicago Press, 1953, p. 157.

2. THE IMPOSSIBLE PALESTINIAN MARTYR STRATEGY

1 In the course of an interview with a reporter from the daily *al-Sharq al-Awsat*, published in London on 21 April 2001, the Grand Mufti of Saudi Arabia declared that suicide attacks were unlawful. This declaration set off a debate in the Arab world about the Palestinian attacks on Israeli civilians. Dyala Hamza has produced an original analysis of these questions in an essay yet to be published, "Intifâda's Fidâ: Suicide or Martyrdom? (Trans)Nationalist Icons, Islamic Consultation and Some Notions of Modern Polity". In addition Farhad Khosrokhavar has contributed to our understanding of the martyr question in Islam in *Nouveaux martyrs d'Allah*, Paris, Flammarion, 2002.

2 In particular Professor Sari Nusseibeh, and several Palestinian deputies including Hannan Ashrawi, Ziad Abou Ziad and Hisham Abd al-Razaq, who called for an end to the attacks on Israeli civilians in June 2002. See MEMRI, Inquiry and Analysis Series, no. 101, http://www.memri.org.

3 On 25 February 1994 an Israeli settler, Baruch Goldstein, entered the Ibrahim Mosque at Hebron and opened fire on the Palestinians who were praying there before being overpowered. 29 Palestinians were killed.

4 Figures given by the Israeli Minister of Foreign Affairs. Human Rights Watch has declared that these attacks killed 130 Israelis and wounded 150 others. Between November 1998 and November 2000 no suicide attacks took place.

⁵　Figures taken from Human Rights Watch. For the same period the Minister of Foreign Affairs registered a higher number, but he did not distinguish between suicide operations and bombs placed under vehicles.

⁶　See Pénélope Larizillière, "Le "martyr" palestinien, nouvelle figure d'un nationalisme en échec", in Alain Dieckhoff and Rémy Leveau, eds, *Israéliens et Palestiniens: la guerre en partage*, Paris, Ballard, 2003.

⁷　Interviews conducted in the Nablus region in April 2001.

⁸　The number of stone throwers killed in the first Intifada was lower. The estimate is one thousand deaths caused by the Israeli Army between 1987 and 1993. For the months of October and November 2000 alone, the figure is 200 Palestinian victims.

⁹　See Rashid Khalidi, *Palestinian Identity: The Construction of Modern National Consciousness*, New York, Columbia University Press, 1977, chpt. 8.

¹⁰　This relative indifference of Palestinians in regard to the Shoah should not be interpreted as anti-Judaism. While it is true that a certain number of Palestinians have been influenced by the revisionist theories developed in Europe, the majority of Palestinians are sufficiently acquainted with Israelis to avoid succumbing to racial fantasies. Yet it is true that as a general rule Arabs do not feel concerned by the question. It is not possible for them to have the same relationship to this tragedy as the Europeans, some of whom were directly responsible for the deportation and the extermination of the Jews.

¹¹　Interview in Bethlehem, June 1996.

¹²　This Arab term means "young man", but the definition is far from precise in terms of age and status. As used here, it refers to the protagonists of the Intifada.

¹³　Interviews with the protagonists themselves, in addition to field observation.

¹⁴　See Laetitia Bucaille, *Gaza: la violence de la paix*, Paris, Presses de Sciences Po, 1998, p. 181.

¹⁵　Excerpts from a text left by Hicham Hamed, an Islamic Jihad militant who blew up his bicycle near the Netzarim colony in the Gaza Strip on 11 November 1994.

¹⁶　Nasra Hassan, "An Arsenal of Believers", *The New Yorker*, 19 November 2001.

¹⁷　See the combined statistics given by Pénélope Larzillière (note 6).

[18] The operations launched by the *shebab* from bases in Zone A (under Palestinian Authority control) are controversial; the inhabitants of the region, who come under both sides' fire, consider them ineffective and uncalled for. Yasser Arafat forbid them.

[19] The enlistment of girls in the ranks of the suicide bombers can be interpreted as a symptom of the process of individualization taking place within Palestinian society.

[20] On the training of the armed forces of Fatah, see the informative article by Jean-François Legrain, "Les Phalanges des martyrs d'Al-aqsa en mal de leadership national", in *Maghreb Machrek*, no. 176, summer 2003, pp. 11-34.

[21] Pénélope Larzillière (note 6).

[22] "The Suicide Bombers", *The New York Review*, 16 January 2003.

[23] Alain Dieckhoff and Rémy Leveau, eds, *Israéliens et Palestiniens: la guerre en partage*, Paris, Balland, 2003.

3. KASHMIRI SUICIDE BOMBERS: 'MARTYRS' OF A LOST CAUSE

[1] *Umm Hamad, Ham Maen Lashkar-i-Tayyeba Ki* ("We, the Mothers of the Lashkar-i-Tayyeba"), Lahore, Markaz Dawa wal-Irshad, 1998. Subsequent quotes without references are from this compilation containing personal accounts by 77 families of "martyrs" and their last wishes.

[2] A personal estimate based on figures from Jihadist organizations, Indian security forces and independent local observers.

[3] In fact they cover two distinct strategies: either the militant accepts, and even desires, to be killed by the enemy, or he kills himself while killing his enemy.

[4] And, one might add, the history of the idea of a "martyr of *jihad*" (which only appears in the Koran in periphrastic form) prompted a proliferation of discursive "mediators". Alfred Morabia, *La notion de Gihad dans l'Islam médiéval, des origines à al-Gazali*, Lille, Université de Lille III, 1975, pp. 408-415.

[5] Seyyed Vali Reza Nasr, *Islamic Leviathan. Islam and the Making of State Power*, Oxford University Press, 2001.

[6] The government has continually limited their access to jobs in the administration. Indeed, in 1989 Muslims (64% of the population) represented only 1.5% of public bank directors and filled only 30% of jobs in the administration. Navnita Chadha Behera, *State, Identity and Violence. Jammu, Kashmir and Ladakh*, New Delhi, Manohar, 2000, p. 154.

7   Lashkar-i-Tayyeba, for example, grew out of a Pakistan *mujahidin* movement, inspired by the Ahl-i-Hadith and the Salafist schools of thought, which was created in the Afghan province of Nuristan shortly before the Soviet withdrawal.

8   Two "martyr cemeteries" in Srinagar are reserved for secessionist militants who have died since 1988.

9   Repeated sixty times since then, they have caused the deaths of 160 members of the Indian security forces and 90 militants. "LeT communication centre busted", *Daily Excelsior* (Jammu), 30 November 2002.

10 Interview with a Lashkar leader, Lahore, October 2002.

11 "What can the Indian Army do against these soldiers who enter its camps ready to die as martyrs?" it wrote in its weekly (*Jihad Times*, 13 November 1999).

12 They represent two-thirds of the "terrorists" killed between 1993 and 2003 (figures from the Indian Ministry of the Interior).

13 The "Line of Control" (the former ceasefire line) separates the Indian part of Kashmir, over 778 km, from the part controlled by Pakistan ("Azad Kashmir", or free Kashmir).

14 *Bharat se ab larenge ham* ("Now we shall fight against India"), Karachi, undated.

15 Interview, head of the Jamaat-i-Islami Jammu&Kashmir, Srinagar, January 2003.

16 "Umer Jan Shahid", *Jehad-e-Kashmir* (Hizb's bi-monthly), 15 November 1999.

17 Muzamil Jaleel, "Nadeem Khateeb: 'I am going at the call of Allah and doing what Allah made our farz'", *Indian Express-Kashmir Live*, 21 October 2001.

18 Interviews, Srinagar, January 2003. For 1988-90, see Behera (note 6), pp. 169-83.

19 Less than 2% of the inhabitants of the Valley think Kashmir should remain part of India, according to a credible poll carried out by the Centre for the Study of Developing Societies in collaboration with the departments of political science at the universities of Jammu and Srinagar (*A Study of Jammu and Kashmir Assembly Elections 2002*, New Delhi, CSDS, 2002).

20 5,000 Kashmiris aged 14 to 70 are still missing after being arrested by the police, the army, or "renegades", a phenomenon which the head of the provincial government only acknowledged publicly in 2002. Jammu&Kashmir Coalition of Civil Society, Peace Initiative, Srinagar, JKCCS, 2002. Added

to these arrests, which Amnesty International cannot observe (since they are not permitted to enter Kashmir), are gang rapes, burned-down houses and everyday harassment by soldiers and the police.

21 Interviews with students from Srinagar, December 2002.

22 Interview, Lahore, October 2002.

23 "Le "martyr" palestinien, nouvelle figure d'un nationalisme en échec", in Alain Dieckhoff and Rémy Leveau, eds, *Israéliens et Palestiniens: la guerre en partage*, Paris, Balland, 2003, pp. 89-116.

24 According to one inhabitant of Srinagar. While in the "martyrs' cemetery" in Idgah, he pointed to a grave – of the most important religious leader in northern Kashmir (Mirwaiz Umar Farooq, killed in 1990) – only a few yards away from that of the man's assassin, a Hizb militant.

25 More or less identically worded "wills" – attributed to various "martyrs" – are a frequent phenomenon.

26 "Le modèle Bassidji", *Cultures et Conflits*, n° 29-30, 1998, pp. 59-118. The Jihadist model is in fact close to that of the young Iranians who were also used as cannon fodder by their government (in the war with Iraq), but it is different as it has not been an instrument of internal repression as well.

27 "Facing the enemy with a rocket launcher on our shoulders, a Kalashnikov in our hands, a bomb tied around our chests! High in the mountains, with the Koran on our lips and faith in our hearts! Oh, the Kashmiri nights and discussions about *Jihad*! Could there be anything more enjoyable in the world?", *Shahadat*, audio cassette from Lashkar-i-Tayyeba, Lahore, Al-Dawa Keset Library, undated.

28 The *mujahidin* "phrasing" is a mixture of language levels where words like "training" – phonetically transcribed in Urdu – are said to be Koranic injunctions.

29 A case reported by a Hizb militant (interview, Lahore, September 2002), about which there is naturally no propaganda literature.

30 Mentioned in Sikand (Yoginder), *Militancy in Kashmir: The Case of the Lashkar-i-Tayyeba*, http://peacemonger.com/edition4/

31 Interview, Lahore, September 2002.

32 "Jihad until the End of Time!" exclaim Lashkar's posters.

33 Such prayers, recited frequently in Pakistan, punctuate the forty days following death and are also considered "non-Islamic" by the Ahl-i-Hadith.

34 Like one mother (the wife of a Jamaat-i-Islami officer) who, barely containing her sorrow, said that before learning of her son's "martyrdom" she saw

him "smiling high up in the sky, wearing clothes the colour of the sky and clouds." Interview, Lahore, October 2002.

[35] As a "martyr's" wounds are thought to smell like musk according to Islamic tradition, Hizb tells the story of the father of one Kashmiri *shahid* who, after obtaining police permission to bury his son in the family village, was struck by the "air fragrant with musk scent" when the body was unearthed. *Jehad-e-Kashmir* (note 16).

[36] Interview, Lahore, October 2002.

[37] In order to make "the emotion of *jihad* so strong inside that he should forget everything – his parents, brothers and sisters – and think only of dying on the Path of Allah." Interview, Hizb militant, Lahore, October 2002.

[38] Ahl-i-Hadith, a reformist movement founded in the 19th century in India, is a small minority in Pakistan and Kashmir. It considers itself responsible for "purging" Islam of devotional practices inspired by Sufism (in particular mediation and worship of saints, defended by the Barelwi movement) and Hinduism, for a return only to the Koran and Hadith.

[39] Even nowadays the Censor Board is banning innocent images, such as that of a banana peel thrown onto an apple on a TV game show – for its "suggestive and obscene" nature!

[40] *Jihad Times*, the Lashkar weekly, 13 November 1999.

[41] Akbar S. Ahmed, "Migration, Death and Martyrdom in Rural Pakistan", in Hastings Donnan and Pnina Werbner, eds, *Economy and Culture in Pakistan. Migrants and Cities in a Muslim Society*, London, Macmillan, 1991, pp. 47-268.

[42] Interview, Lahore, September 2002.

[43] The term *maulwi*, meaning a lesser graduate of a *madrasa*, is used – by extension, and often with a pejorative connotation – to denote anyone who shows outer signs of religiosity or uses religion as a lucrative occupation.

[44] Olivier Roy, *L'échec de l'islam politique*, Paris, Le Seuil, 1992, p. 245.

[45] Furthermore, the process has also been fed by personal experiences. One Lashkar leader asserted that the founder of the organization (born in Simla) lost half of his family in massacres while migrating to Pakistani Punjab. Interview, Lahore, October 2002.

[46] A.H. Nayyar, ed., *The Subtle Subversion. The State of Curricula and Textbooks in Pakistan*. Islamabad, Sustainable Development Policy Institute, 2003, pp. 77-88.

[47] Lashkar claimed 1,600 "martyrs" in ten years, and only 360 families of Hizb "martyrs" have received financial assistance in Pakistan (Interviews with officers from Lashkar and Islami Jamiat-i-Tulaba, Lahore, September 2002). Even adding the 2,500 militants imprisoned in India, the final toll is still low compared to the considerable means employed to mobilize society in their favour.

4. CHECHNYA: MOVING TOWARD ISLAMIC NATIONALISM?

[1] Although the Chechen side understood the agreement as a recognition of its independence, the determination of Chechnya's status was postponed until 2001.

[2] Brian Williams, "Caucasus Belli. The Second Russo-Chechen War, 1999-2002. A Struggle for Freedom or Sub-plot to the War on Terrorism?", *Turkistan Newsletter*, 17 May 2002.

[3] A nationalist combatant during the first war, Basayev gradually developed an increasingly Islamist perspective, describing himself as an "Islamist Che Guevara".

[4] Note that while Palestine also appears as a front for *jihad* on jihadist websites, the reference to martyrdom that one can observe in Palestine itself has little to do with the martyrdom of transnational *jihad*, as it exists within the context of Islamic nationalism: Pénélope Larzillière, "Palestinian 'martyrdom', the new face of failed nationalism", in Alain Dieckhoff and Rémy Leveau, eds, *Israéliens et Palestiniens, la guerre en partage*, Paris, Balland, 2003, pp. 89-116. As shown by Khosrokhavar, although suicide bombings are within the range of actions taken by Islamic nationalists and international jihadists, their frames of reference for justifying such actions are different: nationalism is regarded as sacred in one case, and the transnational *umma* (community) of believers in the other (Farhad Khosrokhavar, *Les Nouveaux Martyrs d'Allah*, Paris, Flammarion, 2002).

[5] See Mikhaïl Roshin, "Islam in Chechnya", in Frédérique Longuet-Marx, ed., *Tchétchénie, la guerre jusqu'au dernier*, Paris, Mille et Une Nuits, 2003, p. 118.

[6] On 23 February 1944, Stalin deported the Chechens to Kazakhstan, accusing them of collaborating with the Nazis. The memory of that deportation has remained central to the Chechens.

[7] A group dance accompanied by prayers and songs.

8   By the term "jihadist" we are referring to international Islamist groups sup-
     porting the Salafist doctrine and associating it with jihadism. By "Wahhabis"
     we mean local Islamist groups supporting Salafism.

9   In this regard it could prove interesting to compare it to the role played by
     political Palestinian Islam as seen in movements such as Hamas. Indeed, the
     identity issue serves the same function here of reinterpreting the national
     struggle and of challenging community decision-making structures.

10   Chechen Committee, *Tchétchénie, dix clés pour comprendre*, Paris, La Décou-
     verte, 2003, p. 37.

11   Alfred Morabia, *Le Gîhad dans l'Islam médiéval*, Paris, Albin Michel, 1993,
     pp. 96 and 110.

12   Roshin (note 5), p. 138.

13   Wahhabism grew out of an alliance between a tribal clan, the Sauds, and a
     religious reformer, Abdul Wahhab (1703-1792). See Olivier Roy, *L'Islam
     mondialisé*, Paris, Le Seuil, 2002, p. 136. This work is published in English
     translation as *Globalised Islam*, London: Hurst, 2004.

14   Roy (note 13), p. 133.

15   On this point, Roy (note 13), p. 141.

16   Chechnya Committee (note 10), p. 36.

17   To quote only a descriptive summary of certain videos in Arabic: *Tchétchénie,
     la destruction d'une nation* (December 1999) shows attacks against civilians,
     the systematic destruction of non-military targets by Russian forces, and am-
     putated young children and babies; *Massacre en Tchétchénie* (October 1999)
     shows massacres perpetrated against women and children by Russian forces;
     Jihad au Daghestan shows attacks by the *jihad* in August and September 1999,
     when Chechen *mujahidin* went to help their Muslim comrades in Dagestan.

18   To take part in combat if the local commander decides the struggle is such
     that women must participate, to support the combatants in the battlefield,
     to raise *mujahidin* children, to engage in physical training, to urge loved ones
     to take part in *jihad*, and to study military medicine.

19   Excerpt from a text presenting itself as an English transcription of a video
     entitled *No Surrender!* It is a dialogue between two women, Hawwaa and
     Luiza, preparing to commit a suicide attack, and their instructor. The docu-
     ment, initially featured on the website www.qoqaz.com, can be found on
     www.terrorisme.net. This website, as well as www.religioscope.com, is
     run by Jean-François Mayer, a professor at the University of Fribourg.

[20] On 23 October 2002 a Chechen commando took several hundred spectators hostage. Russian special forces stormed the building using paralyzing gas. All members of the commando were killed, as were numerous hostages.

[21] A French translation of these declarations can be seen on www.terrorisme. net: Prise d'otages à Moscou (26 octobre 2002).

[22] An example of the impact of this kind of discourse on Palestinian refugees in Lebanon in 1999, in the context of clashes with the Lebanese army, has been analyzed by Bernard Rougier: "A sizeable part of this group became literally immersed in jihadist Islamism, identifying itself with the population of Grozny suffering daily bombings by Russian troops. The timing and the place for the fighting were synchronized with the destruction of Grozny by the Russian troops, and in the feverish minds of those following the fighting in Aïn el-Héloué, the struggle against the Lebanese army was indeed an extension of the Chechen jihad against the Russian army." Bernard Rougier, "Reconstructions identitaires et mobilisations religieuses dans les camps de réfugiés palestiniens au Liban depuis la fin de la guerre (1990-2001)", thesis, Paris, Institut d'études politiques, 2002, pp. 354-5. A young Palestinian from the camp even carried out a suicide attack against the Russian Embassy in Beirut (Rougier, ibid., pp. 355-60).

[23] Bernard Rougier, "Dynamiques religieuses et identité nationale dans les camps de réfugiés palestiniens du Liban", in Jean-Francois Legrain, ed., "En attendant la Palestine", *Maghreb-Machreq*, no. 176, September 2003.

[24] On 11 April 2003, *Le Monde* published an article concerning a report from pro-Russian Chechen authorities sent to "the highest level of State" (i.e. Vladimir Putin). This unpublished document mentioned among other things the execution of one hundred civilians per month throughout 2002, nearly three thousand corpses found in mass graves, kidnappings and torture. On 17 April the Chechen Prime Minister, Anatoli Popov, declared that it was not a "secret report" but rather the results of an inquiry led by the Chechen state prosecutor Viktor Kravchenko. According to him, the text actually mentions three hundred civilian kidnappings involving Russian soldiers, some of whom are already serving time.

[25] Brian Williams, "Unraveling the links between the Middle East and Islamic militants in Chechnya", *Central Asia-Caucasus Analyst*, 12 February 2003, p. 2.

[26] Farhad Khosrokhavar, *L'Islamisme et la Mort*, Paris, L'Harmattan, 1995.

27 For Hamit Bozarslan, eliminating the idea of risk in suicide attacks, in which
    death is certain, is a crucial aspect in the development of sacrificial violence.
    Hamit Bozarslan, *Violence in the Middle East: From Political Contest to Self-Sacri-
    fice*, Princeton, Markus Wiener Publishers, 2004.

28 Laurent Vinatier, "Réflexions prospectives sur l'évolution politique de la
    Tchétchénie", Round table discussion on Chechnya, EHESS-IISMM, 5 May
    2003.

29 The bomb attack on 14 May 2003 carried out during a religious celebration
    seemed to be targeting Ahmed Kadyrov. There were fifteen deaths and one
    hundred and forty wounded. Sources disagree about whether it was a suicide
    attack by one or two women, or a bomb which had been placed inside a
    loudspeaker.

30 Interview with Bleuenn Isambard upon his return from Chechnya in the
    summer of 2003.

31 It would have been impossible to write this chapter without the conversa-
    tions I had with Bleuenn Isambard, Uwe Halbach, Anne Le Huérou, Aude
    Merlin, Frédérique Longuet-Marx, Silvia Serrano, Mairbek Vatchagaev and
    Laurent Vinatier, to whom I would like to extend my thanks.

5. VIOLENCE AGAINST THE SELF: THE CASE OF
A KURDISH NON-ISLAMIST GROUP

1 The term "ultimate" does not have a normative meaning, nor does it aim
   to describe an objective reality (what is dangerous or extreme in fasting for
   two or three days as a protest?). We use this term as a subjective justification made by those carrying it out, who always feel that they are in such a
   deadlock situation, such an impasse, that they cannot use any other means of
   action.

2 Even though fasting to death is more often a tactic used by Turkish radical
   left activists.

3 Luc Boltanski, cited in Memmi 1998, p. 10 even talks of a "somatic culture"
   which "supposes the existence of significant relations or affinities between all
   the physical, symbolic and practical behaviours specific to a group" (*Encyclo-
   paedia universalis*, 1989, p. 606).

4 Here parallels can be drawn between the Kurds from other Middle Eastern
   countries as well as with the Turkish population. The body, and in particular
   hairiness, is part of a power system associated with religion, ethnicity or the
   party, for example in Turkey (Fliche 2000).

5   Johanna Siméant points out the major role the Turks and Kurds played in the hunger strikes by illegal migrants, to the extent of institutionalizing "sweetened tea" strikes to hold out longer, even though doctors consider that this is more dangerous for the hunger strikers (Siméant 1998, p. 302).

6   Such as the case of Abas Amini, an Iranian Kurdish asylum seeker in the UK. After a week's hunger strike, he decided to sew up his lips and eyes, embarking on a thirst strike and finally winning his case. See "Ready to die: the asylum-seeker who says he fled torture and was driven to self-mutilation in Britain", *The Independent*, 28 May 2003.

7   Except in the early 1980s, with in particular photographs of the tortured Mazlum Doıan. See *Kurdistan Report*, No.1, November 1982 and No.3, May 1983.

8   When the wounds appear, it is more often in the manner of an autopsy, whose purpose is generally to discover the "truth". But medical photography is first and foremost interested in the patient and then in the illness (going from the patient to the wound), whereas the PKK seems to have gone from the wound to the militant, which does not encourage mourning, especially if the bodies have no grave or must be buried in joy. See Harding and La Harpe 1998 and Foucault 1963, p. 173.

9   Two women had previously immolated themselves, in Diyarbakır in 1990 and Izmir in 1992.

10 Cf. The letter sent by Zeynep Kınacı (Zilan), author of the first PKK suicide bombing, to Abdullah Öcalan: *Özgür Kadın Hareketi Şehitler Albümü* [Album of the martyrs of the Free Women's Movement] Place of publication unknown (Germany), Jina Serbilind, 2005, p. 26.

11 Social identities, constructed within day-to-day interactions, are understood here as subjective, dynamic perceptions of objectivized social characteristics.

12 In her book, Johanna Siméant devotes several pages to the question of the collective or individual character of the hunger strike (Siméant 1998, pp. 236-40). While she refuses to entrench the dichotomy by claiming that the strikes are primarily a means of creating a collective, she seems above all to be guided by the wish not to enter into a debate of a philosophical, moral or political nature. However, we believe it is possible to avoid this pitfall by examining the individual or collective endorsement of the responsibility for going into action.

[13] In 1995 in Berlin, the death of a Kurdish female member of the PKK was not initially linked to starvation (she died after one week) but to a combination of factors: physical weakness as a result of the hunger strike, the heat and the stress caused by the police action to remove the strikers. The PKK strikes can sometimes bring together several hundred people under one roof.

[14] The number of hunger strike deaths in Turkish prisons ran into the dozens in the 1990s. The PKK gradually dissociated itself from these actions during this decade.

[15] Then it is akin to the feeling of guilt described by Pénélope Larzillière in relation to certain Palestinian martyrs who were socially on their way up at the moment of action. (Larzillière 2001, p. 940).

[16] These attacks caused a number of civilian deaths. Nevertheless, the PKK seems to have considered them as an audience and not as a target.

6. THE DISTINCTIVE DEVELOPMENT OF ISLAMIST VIOLENCE IN ALGERIA

[1] O. Roy, *Globalised Islam*. London: Hurst, 2004.

[2] O. Carlier, "D'une guerre à l'autre, le redéploiement de la violence entre soi", *Confluences Méditerranée*, no. 25, Spring 1998.

[3] L. Martinez, *The Algerian Civil War 1990-1998*, London, Hurst, 2000.

[4] Taghout is the Islamists' word for the state. It is borrowed from the language of the Qu'ran and means the Devil. In the vocabulary of the Islamist movements, it also means the Tyrant, the Oppressor, the "false god" who is worshipped out of fear.

[5] On the massacres in Algeria's contemporary history, see: Ch.-A. Julien, *La conquête et les débuts de la colonisation (1821-1871)*, Paris, PUF, 1979; Y. Bénot, *Massacres coloniaux 1944-1950*, Paris, La Découverte, 1994; M. Hamoumou, *Et ils sont devenus harkis*, Paris, Fayard, 1993; N. Yous, *Qui a tué à Bentalha? Algérie: chronique d'un massacre annoncé*, Paris, La Découverte, 2000.

[6] On the GIA, see A. Grignard, "La littérature politique du GIA, des origines à Djamel Zitouni", in F. Dassetto, ed., *Facettes de l'Islam belge*, Brussels, Bruylant, 2001.

[7] In June 1997, a clandestine newsletter, *El Djemaa*, signed by Mahfoud Assouli, alias Abou el Moundhir, justified the massacres in these words: "To those who accuse us of killing blindly, we reply that we are fighting those traitors who have given themselves to the Taghout.[...] When you hear of

slaughter and throat-slitting in a town or village, know that these people belong to the Taghout."

8   X. Bougarel, *Bosnie: anatomie d'un conflit*, Paris, La Découverte, 1996.

9   *Le Matin*, 11 January 1998.

10 That is why Abderrahmane Moussaoui has no hesitation in writing that "the primary reference, the fundamental referent is not this symbolic place shared by many Muslim countries (The Prophet), but a place/moment which has been made sacred, that of the War of Independence.[...] Both those in power and their opponents base their political theology on war." *La Pensée du Midi*, no. 3, Winter 2000.

11 Qari Saïd is considered as one of the founder members of the GIA. This organization is thought to have been born in Peshawar in 1989 and then to have merged in 1992 with the local GIA under the leadership of Mohamed Allel and Abdelhak Layada.

12 *Le Monde*, 16 June 2000.

13 O. Weber, 'Algérie: culture de la violence, culture du doute et rites sacrificiels', http://pourinfo.ouvaton.org/societe/societeetviolence/cultdela-violence.htm Link doesn't work

14 Chams Benghribil, paper given at CERI, Algeria colloquium, 21 May 2002.

15 *El Tath el Moubine*, 10 June 1994.

16 "They [the GIA] also spread the idea that the people are idolatrous and sometimes Taghout. They are forever counting the sins and little mistakes that can be corrected.[...] This people, which has submitted for centuries, which has proved its allegiance to God, its attachment to its religion and its repudiation of non-believers time and time again through glorious revolutions [...] After all that, it is appalling to want to call this people Taghout, and yet that is what some '*mudjahidin*' reserve for this people who have given them their trust and loyalty." Letter to *Le Moudjahidin*, April 1995.

17 Letter to *Le Moudjahidin*, April 1995.

18 See Habib Souaïdia, *La sale guerre*, Paris, La Découverte, 2001.

19 Michel Wieviorka, *The Making of Terrorism*, University of Chicago Press, 1993, p. 64.

20 "Unlike the units operating under the banner of the GIA, the organization does not resort to "blind" attacks in the urban sector.[...] Recourse to terrorist action causing the death of a civilian, must be, in the minds of the leaders of the GSPC, both exemplary and relatively rare", in "Le GSPC". Jean-Michel Salgon, *Les Cahiers de l'Orient*, no. 62, 2001, pp. 89-93.

21 The Algerian press reports that in November 2001, the authorities suppos-
    edly found a letter from Hassan Hattab, leader of the GSPC, ordering that
    "assistance be given" to Mullah Omar in order to combat "non-believers and
    infidels".

22 *Le Matin*, 27 November 2002.

23 Following the attacks of September 11, 2001, a number of Western coun-
    tries announced they had broken up Algerian Islamist networks.

24 On 27 March 2002, the American Secretary of State announced that the
    GSPC had been added to the list of terrorist organizations on the grounds
    that the GSPC was a "cell of the GIA".

25 Labévière points out that Canada became "the sanctuary" of those who want
    to carry on the *jihad*. He adds that, according to a memo from the Canadian
    intelligence and security services, "more than fifty terrorist groups have ap-
    parently exploited the system on Federal territory": R. Labévière, 'Les ré-
    seaux européens d'islamistes algériens: entre déshérence et reconversion",
    Les Cahiers de l'Orient, no. 62, 2001, pp.133-49.

26 *Jeune Indépendant*, 4 May 2002.

27 F. Khosrokhavar, "Les nouvelles formes de la violence", *Cultures et Conflits*,
    no 29-30, 1997.

28 G. Maïza, in *Le Quotidien d'Oran*, 27 October 2002.

29 P. Conessa (article cited) emphasizes: "In Algeria, the blind massacres of
    women and children perpetrated by the GIA or by the GSPC do not seek
    any political or strategic legitimacy: they have become the method itself of
    the war." In "Al Qaïda, secte millénariste", *Le Monde diplomatique*, January
    2002.

30 H. Touati, *Entre Dieu et les hommes: lettrés, saints et sorciers au Maghreb (17e
    siècle)*, Paris, EHESS, 1994.

7. THE STATE, POLITICAL ISLAM AND VIOLENCE:
THE RECONFIGURATION OF YEMENI POLITICS SINCE 9/11

1   James Der Derian, "In Terrorem: Before and After 9/11", in K. Boothe and
    T. Dunne, eds., *Worlds in Collision*, New York, Palgrave, 2002, p. 103.

2   Steven Simon and Daniel Benjamin, "The Terror", *Survival*, vol. 43, n° 4,
    Winter 2001, p. 5. See also their *The Age of Sacred Terror*, New York, Ran-
    dom House, 2002.

3   Zaheer A. Kazmi, "Discipline and Power: Interpreting Global Islam: A Re-
    view Essay", *Review of International Studies*, n° 30, 2004, p. 245.

[4] See Tarak Barkawi, "The Pedagogy of Small Wars", *International Affairs*, vol. 80, n° 1, January 2004, pp. 25-6.

[5] "US Woos Yemen to Fight Terror Without War", *Washington Post*, 22 October 2003.

[6] Consider the following account of Yemen, typical of Western mainstream journalism: "Along the serpentine road that heads east from the Yemeni capital of Sanaa to the desert, the barrel of a tribe-owned tank peers out over rugged, lawless territory where heavily armed local patriarchs shun government authority and harbour Al-Qaida militants", Jonathan Schanzer, "Sanaa Dispatch: Basket Catch", *The New Republic*, 1 September 2003.

[7] See Mark N. Katz on the "tribal cooperation with Al-Qaida" in "Breaking the Yemen-Al-Qaida Connection", *Current History*, n° 660, January 2003, pp. 40-43.

[8] Olivier Roy, "Neo-Fundamentalism", in After September 11 Archive, Social Sciences Research Council, www.ssrc.org/sept11/essays/roy.htm

[9] Interview with Paul Wolfowitz in "U.S. Sees Battles in Lawless Areas after Afghan War", *New York Times*, 8 January 2002.

[10] The practical modalities of US-Yemen counter-terrorism cooperation encompass provision of military equipment and sending of military experts and trainers, including Special Forces units and Navy SEALs to advise, train and assist Yemeni Special Operations Forces and the counter-terrorist unit within the Central Security Forces; intelligence sharing and the reopening of an FBI office in Sanaa; setting up of a system of computerized cameras at all ports, airports and border crossings, which provides centralized monitoring of people's movements in and out of the country; and a long-term training programme designed for the newly set up Coast Guard, provided with a multinational fleet of boats. Interviews carried out in Sanaa with Western diplomats, August 2003, March-April 2004, December 2005.

[11] See for instance Francis Fukuyama's analysis in terms of "Islamo-fascism" in "History and September 11", in Booth and Dunne (note 1), pp. 32-3. Daniele Archibugi, the prime theorizer of "cosmopolitanism", characterizes "terrorists" as eluding any rational logic, except an "evil criminal" one, and suffering "psychiatric problems": in "Terrorism and Cosmopolitanism", After September 11 Archive, op. cit., www.ssrc.org/sept11/essays/archibugi.htm

[12] Jean-Marc Grosgurin, "La contestation islamiste au Yémen", in Gilles Kepel, ed., *Exils et Royaumes: les appartenances au monde musulman aujourd'hui*, Paris,

FNSP, 1994, pp. 235-50. Paul Dresch and Bernard Haykel, "Stereotypes and Political Styles: Islamists and Tribesfolk in Yemen", *International Journal of Middle East Studies*, vol. 27, n° 4, November 1995, pp. 405-431. Renaud Detalle, "Les islamistes yéménites et l'État: vers l'émancipation?", in Bassma Kodmani-Darwish and May Chartouni-Dubarry, eds., *Les États arabes face à la contestation islamiste*, Paris, Armand Colin-Masson, 1997, pp. 271-98. François Burgat, "Le Yémen islamiste entre universalisme et insularité" and Ludwig Stiftl, "The Yemeni Islamists in the Process of Democratization", both in R. Leveau, F. Mermier and U. Steinbach, eds., *Le Yémen contemporain*, Paris, Karthala, 1999, pp. 221-45 and 247-66.

13 For a similar argument see Bernard Haykel, "Islam and the Struggle Within", bitterlemons-international.org, ed. 8, vol. 1, 28 August 2003.

14 This point borrows from Theda Skocpol's argument about the state: *States and Social Revolutions*, Cambridge University Press, 1979, pp. 14-33, and "Bringing the State Back In: Strategies of Analysis in Current Research", in P.B. Evans, D. Rueschemeyer and T. Skocpol (eds.), *Bringing the State Back In*, Cambridge University Press, 1985, pp. 8, 19-20, 165-6.

15 Quintan Wiktorowicz, "Introduction: Islamic Activism and Social Movement Theory", in Q. Wiktorowicz, ed., *Islamic Activism. A Social Movement Theory Approach*, Bloomington, Indiana University Press, 2004, pp. 13-15.

16 Mohammed M. Hafez and Quintan Wiktorowicz, "Violence as Contention in the Egyptian Islamic Movement", in Wiktorowicz (note 15), pp. 61-71.

17 Argument drawn from Georges Balandier, "Dynamiques 'du dedans' et 'du dehors'", in *Sens et puissance*, Paris, Presses Universitaires de France, 1971, pp. 13-147.

18 Burgat, *L'Islamisme en face*, Paris, La Découverte, 2002, pp. 244-7.

19 Burgat (note 18), 1999, p. 235. Michael Collins Dunn, "Islamist Parties in Democratizing States: A Look at Jordan and Yemen", *Middle East Policy*, vol. 2, n° 2, pp. 16-27.

20 Jillian Schwedler, "The Islah Party in Yemen: Political Opportunities and Coalition Building in a Transitional Polity", in Wiktorowicz, ed. (note15), p. 206.

21 Interview with a Yemeni journalist, Sanaa, 19 October 2005. All interviews were conducted in Sanaa, Yemen, unless otherwise stated.

22 Argument made by Schwedler (note 20).

23 Graham E. Fuller, "Islamists in the Arab World: The Dance Around Democracy", Carnegie Papers, Carnegie Endowment for International Peace, n° 49, September 2004, p. 5.

24 See Burgat, *L'Islamisme à l'heure d'Al-Qaida*, Paris, La Découverte, 2005, Chapter 4.

25 "The terrorists claim they are hurting the West as their enemy, but Yemen is being damaged...Yemen has become their enemy", Dr Abdul Karim al-Iryany, quoted in Peter Willems, "Yemen: the Stakes are Higher", *The Middle East*, March 2003. See also interview with Minister of Interior, Gal al-Alimi, Yemen Saba News Agency, 19 November 2002, and President Saleh's TV speech on the occasion of the 26 September Revolution commemoration, Republic of Yemen TV, 25 September 2003.

26 Port activity decreased by 50% as insurance premiums shot up (300% since October 2002, translating to an additional cost of $150,000 for each ship stopping in Yemen), which results in a loss of $3.8 million per month in oil revenue and transshipment income for the government: "Yemen: the Economic Cost of Terrorism", Fact Sheet, Office of Counterterrorism, Washington, DC, 8 November 2002.

27 Prime Minister Ba-Jammal's words are noticeably laced with the "idea of the state": "The battle is exclusively against terrorists and outlaws, and we all have to work harder to consolidate the state's authority in all parts of the country...to bring all social forces under the sway of law and order". Quoted in Nasser Arrabyee, "Yemen Softens Its Stance", *Al-Ahram Weekly*, n° 566, 27 December 2001.

28 Interview with President Saleh, *al-Mustaqbal*, 8 July 2004. All subsequent Arabic sources cited have been accessed using the BBC Summary of World Broadcasts except where otherwise stated. It is noteworthy that though specifically asked by the Yemenis to treat al-Huthi's movement as "transnational terrorism", the US prefers to classify it as an "internal uprising". Interview with an American diplomat, 17 December 2005.

29 Speeches delivered by President Saleh, Saba News Agency, 9 August and 15 September 2004, 16 April 2005.

30 *Al-Sharq al-Awsat*, 18 September 2004.

31 Whitaker, "Storing Up Credit", *Middle East International*, n° 663, 23 November 2001. Arrabyee, "Profession of Fealty", *Al-Ahram Weekly*, n° 562, 29 November 2001.

32 *Yemen Times*, 31 December 2001 and 21 January 2002.

33 *Yemen Times*, 24 September, 12 and 26 November 2001. The figure given, 14,000 people, refers to the total of those arrested among the "Afghans" since 1996.

34 Detalle (note 12), p. 283.

35 Fred Halliday, "The Third Inter-Yemeni War and its Consequences", *Asian Affairs*, vol. 26, n° 2, June 1995, p. 137.

36 Sheila Carapico, "Yemen and the Aden-Abyan Islamic Army", *Middle East Report*, 18 October 2000.

37 Interview with Yemen's Foreign Minister, al-Qirbi, in *Al-Majallah*, 17 August 2003.

38 His sister married Ali Muhsin al-Ahmar, the President's half-brother, commander of the North West military area and himself ideologically close to the Islamists.

39 Sheikh Hussein Badr ed-Din al-Huthi was a Zaydi cleric and an MP for the party of al-Haqq (1993-1997). He was killed by the armed forces on 10 September 2004, which ended the first campaign.

40 Interview with a Yemeni journalist, 16 October 2005.

41 Interview with a senior government official, 23 November 2005.

42 Interview with the head of a Yemeni NGO, 11 December 2005. NewsYemen, 1 December 2005.

43 See Islah's Third Conference final statement, 1 March 2005, available on www.alsahwa-yemen.net.

44 Stiftl (note 12), p. 265.

45 Dresch and Haykel (note 12), p. 406.

46 Burgat, "Les Élections présidentielles de septembre 1999 au Yémen: du 'pluralisme armé' au retour à la 'norme arabe'", *Monde Arabe Maghreb Machrek*, n° 168, April-June 2000.

47 Dresch and Haykel (note 12).

48 Burgat, "Normalisation au Yémen", *Le Monde Diplomatique*, February 2003, p. 22.

49 Interview with Dr Abdul Karim al-Iryany, former Prime Minister and GPC Secretary General, currently special adviser to the President, 7 March 2004.

50 Al-Anisi, former secretary general of Islah, quoted in Bernard Lefresne, "Les islamistes yéménites et les élections", *Monde Arabe Maghreb Machrek*, n° 141, July-August 1993, p. 36.

[51]   Typology proposed by Burgat in *L'Islamisme en face*, Paris, La Découverte, 2002, p. 113.

[52]   Interview in *Al-Majallah*, 29 June 2003.

[53]   Grosgurin (note 12), pp. 238-9.

[54]   Faris Saqqaf, quoted in Dresch and Haykel (note 12), p. 414. A useful illustration is provided by Laurent Bonnefoy and Fayçal Ibn Cheikh, "Le Rassemblement Yéménite pour la Réforme (Islah) face à la crise du 11 Septembre et à la guerre en Afghanistan", *Chroniques Yéménites* 2001, Sanaa, CEFAS, pp. 169-75.

[55]   Dresch and Haykel (note 12), p. 406.

[56]   See François Burgat and Marie Camberlin, "Révolution: mode d'emploi. Muhammad Mahmud al-Zubayri et les erreurs des Libres", *Chroniques Yéménites* 2001, Sanaa, CEFAS, pp. 107-116.

[57]   Robert D. Burrowes, "The Yemen Arab Republic and the Ali Abdallah Saleh Regime: 1978-1984", *The Middle East Journal*, vol. 39, n° 3, Summer 1985, pp. 287-316.

[58]   Bernard Rougier, "Yémen 1990-1994: la logique du pacte politique mise en échec", in Leveau, Mermier and Steinbach, (note 12), pp. 112-13, 128.

[59]   Interview with a member of Islah, 30 October 2005.

[60]   Interview, *Al-Majallah* (note 52).

[61]   Nazih N. Ayubi, *Over-stating the Arab State*, London, I.B. Tauris, 1995, p. 435.

[62]   Interview with an international diplomat, 29 August 2003.

[63]   Following Yemen's abstention during the UN Security Council's vote on the war on Iraq, 800,000 Yemeni workers were expelled from Saudi Arabia and all financial assistance from the Gulf countries and the United States was suspended.

[64]   For a detailed account of these processes, see Schwedler (note 20), especially pp. 217-23.

[65]   Franck Mermier, "L'Islam politique au Yémen ou la "Tradition" contre les traditions?", *Monde Arabe Maghreb Machrek*, n° 155, January-March 1997, pp. 9-12.

[66]   Arrabyee, "Yemen Report on Terror Receives Mixed Reaction", *Gulf News*, 3 January 2003.

[67]   "Yemenis Go to Third Polls since 1990 amid Mud Slinging over Terror Links", Agence France Presse, 25 April 2003.

68 In addition to Islah, the JMP include the Nasserite, Ba'athist and Socialist parties as well as al-Haqq and the United Popular Front.

69 Interview with a member of Islah, 16 March 2004.

70 Islah made significant gains in Aden and Sana'a. Still, the number of seats it holds has declined constantly, from 62 in 1993, to 53 in 1997 and then 45 in 2003.

71 Interview with Foreign Minister al-Qirbi in *Al-Sharq al-Awsat*, 2 May 2003. The GPC won 240 of 301 seats (including GPC-affiliated independents). The elections were marred by fraud and illegality (underage voting, vote-buying and obstruction by counting commissioners from the ruling party), and by military and police intimidation during counting: National Democratic Institute, April 27, 2003 Parliamentary Elections in Yemen. Final Report.

72 Carapico, "How Yemen's Ruling Party Secured an Electoral Landslide", *Middle East Report*, 16 May 2003. Also Amy Hawthorne, "Yemen's Elections: No Islamist Backlash", *Arab Reform Bulletin*, vol. 1, n° 1, June 2003.

73 The GPC is "a revolving door organization...an agency for the allocation of public offices, with no ideological drive nor distinct political content to substantiate it". Interview with a senior government official, 30 October 2005.

74 Burrowes (note 57), p. 299.

75 *Al-Sharq al-Awsat*, 15 May 2004.

76 President's speech at Ramadan fast-breaking meal, Yemen Saba News Agency, 20 November 2002.

77 Arrabyee, "Yemen Battles Militants", *Gulf News*, 1 July 2003.

78 *Al-Sahwa*, 15 and 23 October 2003. Agence France Presse, 1 November 2003.

79 For the mixed American reaction to this development, see US Department of State, *Patterns of Global Terrorism 2003*, 29 April 2004. Also Schanzer's comment on Yemen's "inconsistency" in the "war on terror" in "Yemen's Al-Qaida Amnesty: Revolving Door or Evolving Strategy?", *PolicyWatch*, n°808, 26 November 2003.

80 Some of the released militants were later identified among the insurgents participating in the "resistance" in Iraq. Interview with a Yemeni journalist, 21 October 2005. United Press International, 13 October 2005.

81 Interview with Foreign Minister, al-Qirbi, in *Al-Sharq al-Awsat*, 9 May 2003. As a further token of reconciliation, the President appointed Salim Saleh Muhammad, a prominent Socialist, as his special adviser in May 2003:

Whitaker, "Magnanimous Gesture", *Middle East International*, n° 701, 30 May 2003.

[82] François Burgat and Mohammed Sbitli, "Les Salafis au Yémen ou...la modernisation malgré tout", *Chroniques yéménites 2002*, Sanaa, CEFAS, p. 144.

[83] *Yemen Observer*, 3 July 2004.

[84] Fuller (note 23), p. 13.

[85] Interview with a Yemeni journalist and member of Islah, 19 August 2003.

[86] *Al-Sahwa*, 13 September 2001. See Schwedler, "Islamist Parties and Regime Responses: Jordan and Yemen", *Middle East Policy*, vol. 9, n° 4, December 2002, pp. 92-3.

[87] *Al-Hayat*, 3 January 2003.

[88] Interviews with various members of Islah, 16 and 19 August 2003, 21 March 2004, 27 and 30 October 2005.

[89] Interview with a member of Islah, 27 October 2005.

[90] Interview with a member of Islah, 30 October 2005.

[91] *Al-Sahwa*, 9 January 2003.

[92] Interview with a member of Islah, 30 October 2005.

[93] Interviews with members of Islah (27 and 30 October), a Nasserite cadre (16 November) and a prominent Unionist (18 November) and Socialist leaders (18 December), 2005.

[94] Interview with a member of Islah, 16 August 2003.

[95] Whitaker, "Islamist targets", *Middle East International*, 24 January 2003.

[96] Interview with a senior government official, 30 October and 17 November 2005. Noteworthy is the fact that, except for its brief closure in the wake of 9/11, al-Iman was never jeopardized despite serious reservations expressed by the Americans.

[97] Interview with a member of Islah, 27 October 2005. See "Al-Zindani's attacks own party member (Qahtan) and praises President Saleh", *NewsYemen*, 21 November 2005.

[98] Interview with a member of Islah, 21 October 2005. *Yemen Times*, 5 January 2006.

[99] For instance, the JMP's political reform initiative was labelled as "treason" by the GPC: *NewsYemen*, 30 November 2005.

[100] It is a widely accepted fact among the opposition itself that the JMP is "a weak assemblage of disparate parties", "a congregation of elites speaking from an ivory tower", an "opposition that does not oppose the regime" etc.

Interviews with prominent members of Islah, the YSP, the Nasserite and Unionist Parties, Sana'a, October-December 2005.

101 Interview with a senior GPC official, 22 December 2005.

102 "Islah Party demanded to be more democratic by its own members", *News Yemen*, 3 November 2005.

103 Wording used by Dr Condoleezza Rice, Ninth Public Hearing, 9/11 Commission, 8 April 2004, p. 76 of transcript, www.9-11commission.gov/archive/hearing9/index.htm

104 Clement M. Henry and Robert Springborg, *Globalization and the Politics of Development in the Middle East,* Cambridge University Press, 2001, pp. 99-100.

105 Carapico, *Civil Society in Yemen*, Cambridge University Press, 1998, p. 17.

SELECTED BIBLIOGRAPHY

Ahmed, Rifaat Sayed. *The Militant Prophet*. London: Riad El-Rayyes Books, vol. 1, 1991.

Arkoun, Mohammed. *L'islam, morale et politique*. Paris: Desclée de Brouwer, 1986.

Benslama, Fethi. *La psychanalyse à l'épreuve de l'islam*. Paris: Aubier, 2002.

Bloom, Mia. *Dying to Kill: The Allure of Suicide Terror*. New York: Columbia University Press, 2005.

Bozarslan, Hamit. *Violence in the Middle East: From Political Struggle to Self Sacrifice*, Princeton: Markus Wiener Publishers, 2004.

Brumberg, Daniel. *Moyen-Orient: l'enjeu démocratique*. Paris: Michalon, 2004.

Bucaille, Laetitia. *Gaza: la violence de la paix*, Paris: Presses de Sciences Po, 1998.

Burgat, François. *L'islamisme au Maghreb*. Paris: Karthala, 1988.

Charif, Mohamed. *Islam et liberté*. Paris: Albin Michel, 1999.

Charnay, Jean-Paul. *L'Islam et la guerre: de la guerre juste à la révolution sainte*. Paris: Fayard, 1986.

Comité Tchétchénie, *Tchétchénie, dix clés pour comprendre*, Paris: La Découverte, 2003.

Coolsaet, Rik. *Le mythe al Qaida: le Terrorism symptôme d'une société malade*. Bierges, Belgium: Editions Mols, 2004.

Dieckhoff, Alain and Rémy Leveau, eds, *Israéliens et Palestiniens: la guerre en partage*. Paris: Galland, 2003.

Ford, Franklin L. *Le meurtre politique. Du tyrannicide au terrorisme.* Paris: PUF/histoires, 1997.

Gambetta, Diego., ed., *Making Sense of Suicide Missions.* Oxford University Press, 2005.

Hafez, Mohammed. *Why Muslims Rebel? Repression and Resistance in the Islamic World.* London: Lynne Rienner Publishers, 2003.

Huband, Mark. *Warriors of the Prophet.* Boulder, CO: Westview Press, 1998.

Kepel, Gilles. *Jihad. Expansion et déclin de l'islamisme.* Paris: Gallimard, 2000.

Kepel, Gilles. *Du Jihad à la Fitna.* Paris: Bayard, 2005.

Khosrokhavar, Farhad. *L'islamisme et la mort.* Paris: l'Harmattan, 1995.

Khosrokhavar, Farhad. *Les Nouveaux martyrs d'Allah.* Paris: Flammarion, 2002.

Martinez, Luis. *La guerre civile en Algérie,* Paris: Karthala, 1998 (trans. *The Algerian Civil War, 1990-1998.* London: Hurst, 2000).

Meddeb, Abdelwahab, *The Malady of Islam.* New York: Basic Books, 2003.

Morabia, Alfred. *Le gîhad dans l'islam médiéval.* Paris: Albin Michel, 1993.

Navnita Chadha Behera, *State, Identity and Violence. Jammu, Kashmir and Ladakh.* New Delhi: Manohar, 2000.

Nayyar, Abdul Hameed., ed., *The Subtle Subversion. The State of Curricula and Textbooks in Pakistan.* Islamabad: Sustainable Development Policy Institute, 2003.

Roy, Olivier. *L'échec de l'islam politique.* Paris: Le Seuil, 1992.

———. *L'Islam mondialisé,* Paris: Le Seuil, 2002 (trans. *Globalised Islam.* London: Hurst, 2004).

Sageman, Marc. *Understanding Terror Networks.* Philadelphia: University of Pennsylvania Press, 2004.

Schelling, Thomas, *The Strategy of Conflict,* London, Oxford University Press, 1960.

Sivan, Emmanuel. *Mythes politiques arabes.* Paris: Fayard. 1995.

Wright, Robin. *The Sacred Rage.* New York: Linden Press/Simon & Shuster, 1985.

Seyyed Vali Reza Nasr, *Islamic Leviathan. Islam and the Making of State Power,* Oxford University Press, 2001.

Stern, Jessica. *Terror in the Name of God. Why Religious Militants Kill?* New York: HarperCollins, 2003.

Wieviorka, Michel. *Sociétés et Terrorisme.* Paris: Fayard, 1988.

Wiktorowicz, Quintan., ed. *Islamic Activism. A Social Movement Theory Approach.* Indiana University Press, 2004.

Articles

Ahmed, Akbar S. "Migration, Death and Martyrdom in Rural Pakistan", in Hastings Donnan and Thomas M. Wilson, eds, *Economy and Culture in Pakistan. Migrants and Cities in a Muslim Society,* London: Macmillan, 1991, pp. 247-68.

Atran, Scott. "Combating Al-Qaida's Splinters". *Washington Quarterly,* vol. 27, no. 3, pp. 65-113.

Beeman, William O. "Terrorism: Community Based or State Supported?", *Arab-American Affairs,* no. 16, Spring 1986, pp. 29-36.

Bloom, Mia. "Ethnic Conflict, State Terror and Suicide Bombing in Sri Lanka", *Civil Wars,* no. 1, 2003, pp. 54-68.

Carlier, Omar. "D'une guerre à l'autre, le redéploiement de la violence entre soi", *Confluences Méditerranée,* no. 25, Spring 1998.

Grignard, Alain. "La littérature politique du GIA, des origines à Djamel Zitouni", in F. Dassetto, ed., *Facettes de l'Islam belge,* Brusels: Bruylant, 2001.

Kerrou, Mohamed. "Blasphème et apostasie en Islam". In *Monothéismes et Modernités.* Tunis: OROC/Friedrich-Naumann Stifting, 1996, pp. 117-204.

Khosrokhavar, Farhad. "Le modèle Bassidji", *Cultures et Conflits,* no. 29-30, 1998, pp. 59-118.

Krämer, D. "La morale du Hezbollah et sa logique", in *Maghreb Machrek,* January-March 1988, pp. 39-59.

Larzillière, Pénélope. "Le "martyr" palestinien, nouvelle figure d'un nationalisme en échec", in A. Dieckhoff and Rémy Leveau, eds, *Israéliens et Palestiniens: la guerre en partage,* Paris: Balland, 2003.

Leca, Jean and Yves Schmeil. "Clientélisme et néo-patrimonialisme dans le monde arabe", *International Political Science Review* 1983, vol. 4, no.4, pp.455-94.

Legrain, Jean-François. "Les Phalanges des martyrs d'Al-Aqsa en mal de leadership national", in *Maghreb Machrek*, no. 176, Summer 2003, pp. 11-34.

Lewis, Bernard. "What Went Wrong?" *The Atlantic Monthly*, Vol. 289, no. 1, January 2002.

Pape, Robert. "The Strategic Logic of Suicide Terrorism", *American Political Science Review*, vol. 97, no. 3, August 2003.

Roshin, Mikhail. "L'islam en Tchétchénie", in Frédérique Longuet-Marx, ed., *Tchétchénie, la guerre jusqu'au dernier*, Paris: Mille et Une Nuits, 2003, p. 118.

Rougier, Bernard. "Dynamiques religieuses et identité nationale dans les camps de réfugiés palestiniens du Liban", in Jean-Francois Legrain, ed., "En attendant la Palestine", *Maghreb-Machreq*, no. 176, September 2003.

Roussillon, Alain. "Changer la société par le jihad". In *Le phénomène de la violence politique: Perspectives comparatistes et paradigme égyptien*. Le Caire: CEDEJ, 1994, pp. 295-319.

Sikand, Yoginder. "Militancy in Kashmir: The Case of the Lashkar-e-Tayyeba", http://peacemonger.com/edition4.

Williams, Brian. "Caucasus Belli. The Second Russo-Chechen War, 1999-2002. A Struggle for Freedom or Sub-plot to the War on Terrorism?" *Turkistan Newsletter*, 17 May 2002.Williams, Brian. "Unravelling the Links between the Middle East and Islamic Militants in Chechnya", *Central Asia-Caucasus Analyst*, 12 February 2003, p. 2.

INDEX